A GREEN GUIDE TO
COUNTRY CRAFTS

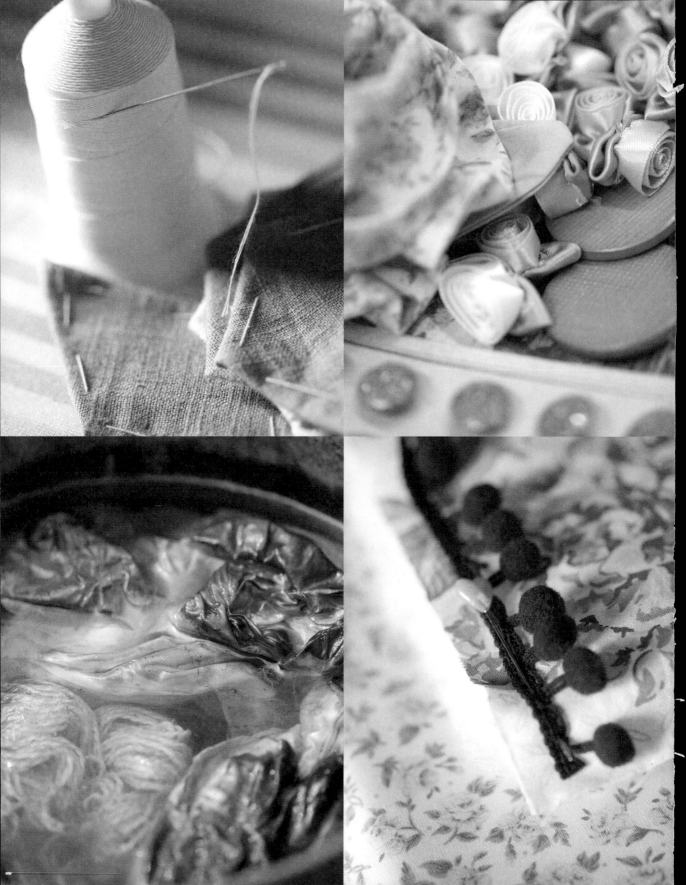

A GREEN GUIDE TO
COUNTRY CRAFTS

35 beautiful step-by-step projects

NICOLA GOULDSMITH AND JACQUELINE MANN
OF HALFPENNY HOME

CICO BOOKS
LONDON NEW YORK

Published in 2011 by CICO Books
An imprint of Ryland Peters & Small

20–21 Jockey's Fields
London WC1R 4BW

519 Broadway, 5th Floor
New York, NY 10012

10 9 8 7 6 5 4 3 2 1

A CIP catalog record for this book is available from the
Library of Congress and the British Library.

ISBN: 978 1 907563 17 1

Printed in China

Editor: Helen Ridge
Designer: Louise Leffer
Photographer: Gavin Kingcome

Contents

Introduction

We were brought together by mutual friends who said they always knew we would get on and work well together—they were right! We have a shared belief that the enjoyment of making something is as important as the end result, and that making a gift for a loved one is something that you cannot put a price on. This forms the basis of what we do at Halfpenny Home and what we share with you here in *A Green Guide to Country Crafts*.

   In writing this book our aim was, of course, to create something that you'd want to pick up and read, but we also wanted to create a visual treat that would inspire and excite—a book that

you'd want to refer to again and again. In all the projects in this book, we have tried to take the mystery out of craft and encourage you all to have a go, even if you think you can't—believe us, you can! It's not about being perfect or following fashion, nor is it about having a host of expensive equipment. It's about taking what you have—finding the beauty in the under-valued, unused, and forgotten items and using them to create something that you will treasure and that is personal to you.

We believe there's a whole generation, maybe two, that have missed out on the excitement and fulfillment that comes from

making things. Thankfully, that's changing now and people are realizing how brilliant it is to make stuff! Sadly, many people have lost the opportunity to obtain these skills from their grandparents and parents and we want to try, in some small way, to bridge that gap. We know from all our lovely Halfpenny Home friends what a difference craft can make to people's lives. It opens up a whole new world with endless possibilities—not just from learning new skills and creating beautiful things, but from making friends too! And although we understand perfectly that time is precious, we promise you that once you start, you will be hooked! It's the best antidote to

stress that we know! We want to fly the banner for handmade, to celebrate it and show that handmade most definitely does not mean second-rate. We want craft to be seen as art, which we truly believe it is, and most of all we want to equip you with the knowledge and confidence to have a go yourself. You will be amazed at what you can create, and how wonderful crafting will make you feel.

Nicola and Jacqueline

Chapter One

Soapmaking

Traditional cold process soapmaking was once much more commonplace than it is today and, although in our recipes we have used cocoa butter, coconut oil, and olive oil to replace the lard that would have been used traditionally, the process of using lye (caustic soda solution) to turn fats into soap is just the same. Using a handheld blender to mix the solution, instead of stirring by hand, makes the soapmaking process much quicker and a lot less likely to go wrong!

In this chapter we show you how to make a basic cocoa butter soap, and shampoo bars that can be adapted to suit your hair type, along with some soaps—a rose and geranium soap and a fun chocolate mint layer soap—that include cleansing clays. Handmade soap, cut into bars and wrapped in brown paper tied with pretty ribbon, makes a lovely gift. Attaching a parcel tag with a handwritten list of the ingredients adds a personal touch.

The basics

Making soap using the "cold process" method requires lye (caustic soda solution) in order to turn a combination of oils into soap (saponify). Soapmaking at home is very similar to cooking. The utensils you need are to be found in most kitchens, although make sure that they will no longer be used for preparing food. You will also need a microwave oven. Accurate measuring is the key to successful soapmaking, which means that a good set of digital kitchen scales is essential.

The following recipes will fill a 2-pint (1-liter) mold, or you could use several smaller molds, such as silicon muffin pans (cupcake cases). Line rigid molds, such as plastic tubs, with plastic wrap (clingfilm), to make it easier to remove the soap.

The soap is ready to cut into bars after 24 hours. Although safe to use immediately, it will be quite harsh and drying to the skin. It is better to lay the bars out on a rack in an airy place for four weeks, turning them regularly to help them cure and dry. The soap will then be milder and last longer.

Using Essential Oils

Some of the recipes contain essential oils, which must be of a good quality. Anyone pregnant should seek medical advice before using these particular soaps. Label any soaps containing essential oils clearly.

Soapmaking—the rules!

The soap recipes in this book are intended for non-commercial production only. However, if you get the soapmaking bug and think that you would like to sell your soaps, there are a few things you should be aware of before going into business.

According to the Cosmetic Products (Safety) Regulations 2004, any soaps or cosmetics sold in the UK and the rest of the EU, must have had a safety assessment carried out by a chemist. The products must also be labeled correctly. The regulations apply to anyone producing soap for sale, even if you're making only a few bars for friends or for selling at a craft fair. A lot of information about these regulations is available on the internet, and some useful web addresses are given on pages 188–189. Interestingly, no such regulations exist in the United States.

Making lye

The lye (caustic soda solution) has to be made first so that it cools down to room temperature before you can use it. Caustic soda can cause nasty injuries if it is not handled carefully, so always wear long sleeves, gloves, and safety glasses in case of splashes, and work in a well-ventilated area (also read the Precautions box on the opposite page before you begin). Label containers of lye clearly and keep them out of the reach of children and pets. This recipe makes the right amount of lye for the Cocoa butter soap recipe (see page 18). Working out how much caustic soda to use with different combinations of oils is quite complicated, but you can find lye calculators online that enable you to invent some soap recipes of your own.

You will need

6¾oz/190g distilled water
2½oz/70.6g caustic soda

Equipment
Plastic pitcher (jug) with a lid, clearly marked "Lye" ("Caustic soda solution")
Digital kitchen scale
Small bowl
Gloves and safety glasses
Silicon spatula

1 Place the pitcher (jug) on the scale and press the tare button to reset the scale to zero. Weigh out the distilled water and place the pitcher in the refrigerator to cool down.

2 Place the bowl on the scale and press the tare button. Put on the gloves and safety glasses. Very carefully weigh out the caustic soda. Put the lid back on the caustic soda container and store safely.

3 Remove the pitcher of water from the refrigerator. Gently pour the caustic soda into the water—the solution will get hot but not as hot as it would if the water had not been cooled beforehand. Do not inhale the fumes. Stir with the spatula until all the caustic soda has dissolved.

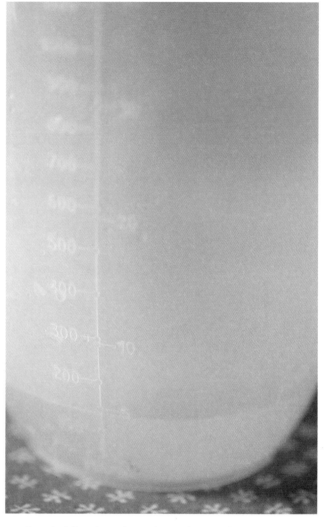

4 Place the lid on the pitcher and set aside in a safe place to cool—it needs to be around 98° F/37° C before it can be used.

PRECAUTIONS

Always add caustic soda to water, NEVER water to caustic soda, as this will cause the mixture to erupt suddenly and violently, which could lead to serious chemical burns. When caustic soda is added to distilled water, a chemical reaction takes place that causes the mixture to heat up. To keep the solution as cool as possible, we place the water in a refrigerator first. Deal with spills immediately before the lye damages work surfaces. Clean splashes with a cloth soaked in vinegar, to help neutralize the lye.

Cocoa butter soap

This soap is gorgeous just as it is, but it can also be adapted quite easily to make exfoliating soaps, clay soaps, and shampoo bars. Before you start, make sure that all your utensils are clean and the mold is ready. This is because a chemical reaction will take place as soon as the oils and lye are mixed, and you need to work quickly after this point. You should not use aluminum or plastic bowls for the mixing, as they can react with the lye or absorb the oils. We used Pyrex, which is heatproof glass and can be placed in the microwave oven.

You will need

7oz/200g coconut oil
5¼oz/150g cocoa butter
3½oz/100g olive oil
1¾oz/50g castor oil
Lye (caustic soda solution)
(see pages 14–15)

Equipment
Large Pyrex or heatproof glass bowl
Digital kitchen scale
Microwave oven
Silicon spatula
Gloves and safety glasses
Thermometer
Handheld blender
2-pint/1-liter mold—if the mold is
rigid, line it with plastic wrap
(clingfilm)
Plastic wrap (clingfilm)
Old towel
Sharp knife, for cutting into bars

1 The easiest way to measure out the soap ingredients is with the tare feature. Place the bowl on the scale and press the tare button to reset the scale to zero. Measure out the coconut oil into the bowl and press the button. Add the cocoa butter, followed by the olive oil, then the castor oil, resetting the scale to zero after each ingredient.

2 Place the bowl in the microwave oven and heat the oils gently using 30-second bursts until the hard oils (coconut and cocoa butter) have melted into the liquid oils. Remove the bowl after each burst, and stir with the spatula.

3 Put on your gloves and safety glasses, and cover your arms. Measure the temperatures of the lye and the oils. Both need to be around 98° F/37° C.

4 Slowly and carefully pour the lye into the bowl of melted oils.

5 Stir the mixture gently with the handheld blender without turning it on, to start combining the oils and the lye.

6 Still stirring, switch on the blender for short bursts. The mixture will start to thicken. Keep stirring in between bursts.

7 Check for trace—the point at which the oils and lye have combined successfully to make soap—by lifting the switched-off blender out of the mixture and letting some of it dribble back into the bowl. If it leaves a trail on the surface, you have reached trace. Take care not to overdo the blending—if the mixture becomes too thick, it will be difficult to pour.

CLEANING YOUR PITCHER

Once you have emptied the pitcher (jug) of lye, place it in a basin full of clean water. This will dilute any remaining lye and help make cleaning up later much safer.

8 Pour the soap mixture into the mold, using the spatula to scrape any remaining mixture out of the bowl and to smooth the surface. Remember that the soap mixture is still caustic at this stage, so do not touch it with your bare hands.

9 Cover the mold with plastic wrap (clingfilm), then wrap loosely in the towel. The towel insulates the soap, which helps the saponification and curing process. Let the soap harden for 24 hours. Remove from the mold, then cut into bars. Lay out the bars, uncovered, on a rack to cure for four weeks before using.

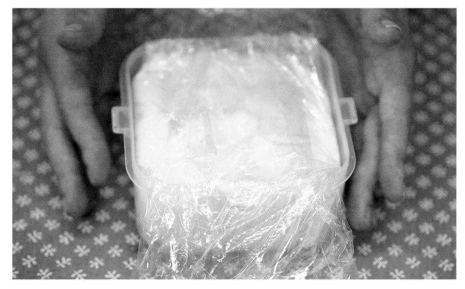

Honey and oat scrub

Honey has so many healing properties that it makes perfect sense to include it in a soap. In this recipe, it has been combined with oats, which have a softening effect on the skin and act as a gentle exfoliator. The recipe also contains bergamot FCF essential oil. FCF indicates that the furocoumarin, a phototoxic ingredient, has been removed, which means the oil is suitable for skin products. Bergamot has a deodorizing, soothing, as well as an uplifting effect, which makes this soap a good pick-me-up. Anyone pregnant should seek medical advice before using this soap because it contains essential oils. It isn't necessary to insulate the finished soap with a towel, as the sugar in the honey generates enough heat to aid saponification.

You will need

Ingredients used for the Cocoa butter soap recipe (see page 18)
1 tbsp runny honey
$\frac{1}{5}$oz/5g bergamot FCF essential oil
$\frac{1}{5}$oz/5g chamomile essential oil
Small cup of oats

Equipment
Equipment used for the Cocoa butter soap recipe (see page 18), except for the towel (see above)

1 Follow steps 1–7 of the Cocoa butter soap recipe on pages 18–20. Do not overheat as this will spoil the soap. Pour in the honey, which should be at room temperature.

2 Add the bergamot FCF and the chamomile essential oils to the mixture and blend together well using a metal spoon.

4 Pour the mixture into the mold and smooth the top with a spatula.

3 Mix the oats into the mixture. Alternatively, wait and sprinkle them on the top of the mixture after pouring it into the mold.

5 Cover the mold with plastic wrap (clingfilm) and let the soap harden for 24 hours. Remove from the mold, then cut into bars. Lay out the bars, uncovered, on a rack to cure for four weeks before using.

Rose and geranium soap

The addition of good-quality rose and geranium essential oils, along with vitamin E oil and pink clay, make this soap especially suitable for mature skins. This is a pretty soap—the pink layer is swirled with the white layer to create a marbled effect, which is seen when you cut the soap into bars. This soap looks great set in a round cake pan (tin) lined with plastic wrap (clingfilm) and then cut into slices. Anyone pregnant should seek medical advice before using these soaps because they contain essential oils. Always wear gloves and safety glasses, and cover your arms whenever you are working with the lye (caustic soda solution).

You will need

Ingredients used for the Cocoa butter soap recipe (see page 18)

1 tbsp pink clay

⅓oz/10g geranium essential oil

⅕oz/5g rose essential oil

2 tbsp vitamin E oil

Equipment

Equipment used for the Cocoa butter soap recipe (see page 18)

Tablespoon

Small bowl, for reserving the oils

Large bowl

Chopstick or skewer

1 Follow steps 1 and 2 of the Cocoa butter soap recipe on pages 18–19. Take out two tablespoons of the melted oils and put them in the small bowl. Mix the pink clay with the reserved oils and mix well until you have a runny paste. Set the bowl aside.

2 Continue to follow the Cocoa butter soap recipe, steps 3–7 on pages 19–20, making sure that you are wearing gloves and safety glasses, and your arms are covered. Once the soap mixture reaches trace, add the essential oils and the vitamin E oil, and blend.

4 Pour the pink soap mixture into a prepared mold.

3 Pour half the soap mixture into a bowl and stir in the pink clay paste. Remember that the soap mixture is still caustic at this stage, so do not touch it with your bare hands.

5 Pour the remaining mixture into the mold, straight onto the pink layer. Stir gently with a chopstick or skewer to create the swirls.

6 Cover the mold with plastic wrap (clingfilm) and wrap loosely in a towel to insulate. Leave undisturbed for 24 hours to harden, then cut into bars. Lay out the bars, uncovered, on a rack for four weeks to cure before using. Even though this soap looks good set in an ordinary plastic container, you could also set it in an old cake pan (tin) lined with plastic wrap. Making a circular soap means that you can cut it into cake-shaped slices!

FINISHING TOUCH

For a lovely, thoughtful gift, "serve" a slice of your handmade soap on a pretty vintage plate.

Shampoo bars

Adding your own choice of a good-quality essential oil to this recipe means that you can make shampoo bars to suit any hair type (see page 31). Setting the soap mixture in silicon cupcake molds means that the bars are the perfect size to use. Anyone pregnant should seek medical advice before using shampoo bars containing essential oils. Always wear gloves and safety glasses, and cover your arms whenever you are working with the lye (caustic soda solution).

You will need

Lye (caustic soda solution), made up
as on pages 14–15 but with
2¹⁄₃oz/66.2g of caustic soda instead
of 2¹⁄₂oz/70.6g
7oz/200g coconut oil
5¹⁄₄oz/150g avocado oil
3¹⁄₂oz/100g jojoba oil
1³⁄₄oz/50g castor oil
Good-quality essential oil
(see page 31)

Equipment
Equipment used for the Cocoa
butter soap recipe (see page 18),
substituting silicon muffin pans
(cupcake cases) for the mold, to make
individual bars if desired
Slotted spoon

1 Follow steps 1–7 of the Cocoa butter soap recipe on pages 18–19, substituting the oils in that recipe with the coconut, avocado, jojoba, and castor oils listed on the left.

2 When the mixture reaches trace, stir in your chosen essential oil with a slotted spoon.

VARIATIONS

To create your shampoo bar, use a good-quality
essential oil. Choose from the following:

$\frac{1}{2}$oz/15g chamomile, for fine to normal hair

$\frac{1}{2}$oz/15g peppermint, for dry hair

$\frac{1}{3}$oz/10g lemon, for oily hair

$\frac{1}{2}$oz/15g lavender, for sensitive scalps

$\frac{1}{3}$oz/10g rosemary, for dark hair

3 Pour the mixture into the mold. Cover with plastic wrap (clingfilm), then wrap loosely in the towel to insulate. Let the soap harden for 24 hours. Remove the soap from the mold, cut into slices if necessary, and lay out, uncovered, on a rack for four weeks to cure before using. Stack two soaps together and tie with string for a pretty gift.

Chocolate mint soap

This fun soap contains real cocoa powder and, although it is chocolatey, it doesn't make you smell of chocolate! The peppermint-green layer is made by adding green clay, which helps to rid the skin of impurities. Always wear gloves and safety glasses, and cover your arms when working with lye (caustic soda solution). Anyone pregnant should seek medical advice before using soap containing essential oils.

You will need

Ingredients used for the Cocoa
butter soap recipe (see page 18)
1 tbsp green clay
1 tbsp cocoa powder
½oz/15g peppermint essential oil

Equipment
Equipment used for the Cocoa
butter soap recipe (see page 18)
Tablespoon
2 small bowls
1 large bowl

1 Follow steps 1 and 2 of the Cocoa butter soap recipe on pages 18–19. Reserve four tablespoons of the melted oils, shared between two small bowls.

2 With a spoon, mix the green clay in a bowl or pan with two tablespoons of the reserved oil, then stir well to make it into a runny paste. Do the same with the cocoa powder and the remaining two tablespoons of oil. Set the bowls aside.

4 Divide the mixture by putting some into another bowl. The mixture does not have to be divided evenly—we used a third of the mixture for the mint layer and the remaining two-thirds for the chocolate layer.

3 Continue to follow the basic soap recipe, steps 3–7 on pages 19–20, making sure that you are wearing gloves and safety glasses, and your arms are covered. Once the soap mixture reaches trace, add the peppermint essential oil and blend together.

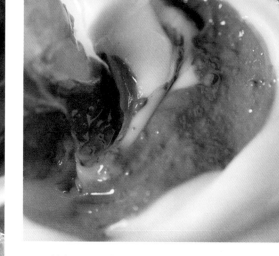

6 Add the green clay paste to the smaller portion of the soap mixture and stir or blend thoroughly until well mixed.

5 Add the cocoa paste to the larger portion of the soap mixture and stir or blend thoroughly. Pour the mixture into a prepared mold.

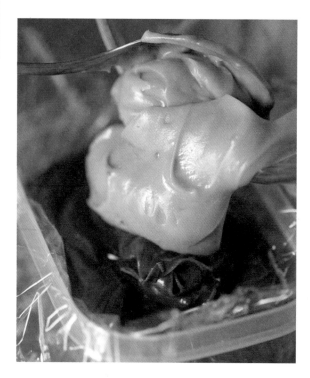

7 Pour the mint layer carefully over the cocoa layer already in the mold.

8 Cover the mold with plastic wrap (clingfilm), then wrap loosely in the towel to insulate. Let the soap harden for 24 hours. Remove the soap from the mold, then cut into bars with the knife.

USING A BLENDER

There is no need to clean the blender between mixing the "mint" and the "chocolate" layers (see step 2)—the green clay will just get mixed in with the cocoa powder, and won't spoil the look of the soap.

9 Lay out the bars, uncovered, on a rack to cure for four weeks before using.

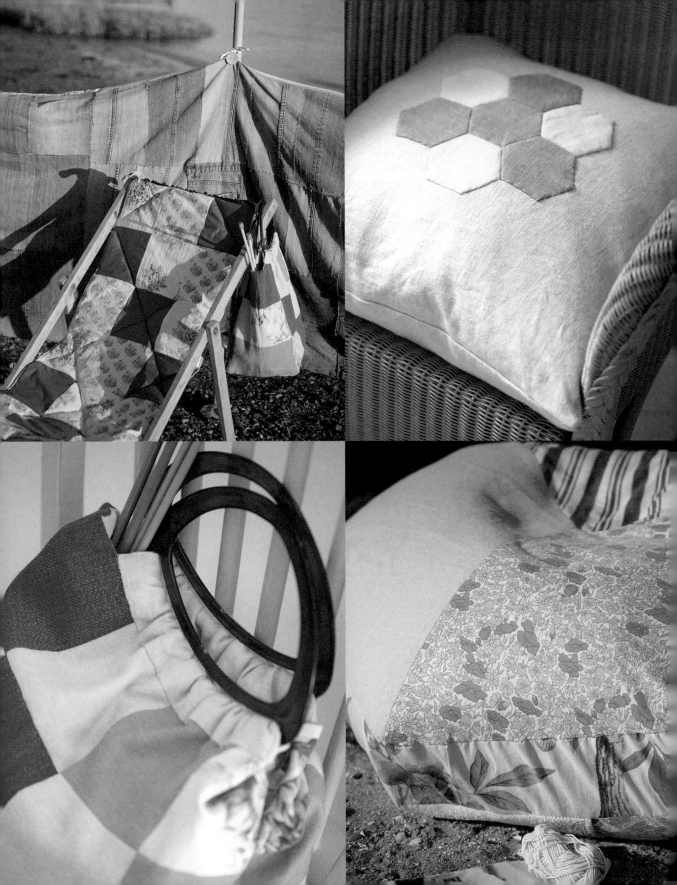

Chapter Two
Patchwork & Quilting

Patchwork has been used for hundreds of years as a way of recycling and reusing fabric. In the past, even the tiniest scrap of fabric would not have been thrown away—to do so would have been considered far too wasteful. Most antique patchwork quilts that you see today have been fashioned from fabrics that had already served their original purpose of clothing a body. They may have even been altered again and again to fit progressively smaller bodies until, finally, the fabric had worn much too thin to be made into yet another garment. It would then end up in the rag bag!

In this chapter we show you how to make a handy knitting bag using bright linens and faded floral fabric, and use traditional techniques to add some patchwork motifs to plain cushion covers in the appliquéd cushions project. The denim windbreak is a fun way to use up all those old pairs of jeans that you couldn't bear to throw away. You can enjoy picnics in comfort on a patchwork beanbag and smarten up an old deckchair with the quilted deckchair cover.

Basic techniques

In English-style patchwork the fabric pieces are basted (tacked) onto paper or card shapes that have been cut out using a template as a guide. After the shapes have all been basted to their papers, the pieces are hand-stitched together using a whip stitch. Patchwork sewn together using the American-style technique uses a slightly different process as there is no need for the papers. Using a template as a guide, the shapes are marked directly onto the fabric. To join the pieces, the lines need to be matched before being sewn together either by hand or machine.

The method of sewing the patches together is referred to as piecing, and after the top of a quilt is pieced together, then the quilting can begin. Quilting simply means that you are joining three layers of fabric by stitching—or "tufting"—them together. The three layers are made up of the quilt top, batting (wadding), and a backing fabric.

When planning your patchwork projects, remember to put similar weights of fabrics together, and avoid mixing man-made fibers such as polyester, with natural fibers like cotton or linen.

The patchwork shown on the opposite page belongs to a friend of mine. It was made by her great-great grandmother from scraps salvaged from old dresses and shirts. Very sadly, it was never finished and turned into a quilt. It has been made in English-style patchwork—you can still see some of the original basting stitches that held the papers in place.

Left: English-style patchwork—the fabric pieces are basted onto paper or card shapes. In American-style patchwork, the pieces are joined without the need for the backing papers.

Below: Stitching together squares with a sewing machine is a quick way to produce a piece of patchwork.

Appliquéd cushions

This is a very good project for getting started with English patchwork because the piecing of the patches is quick to do and the end result is so attractive. We've used a plain natural linen cushion cover as the background and added the patchwork patterns in two of the most commonly seen shapes: hexagons and diamonds. Hexagons set out in this way are known as the granny's garden pattern, while the diamonds are called the star pattern.

You will need

Template (see page 184)
Tracing paper
Pencil
Lightweight card (greetings card or postcard weight)
Scissors
Scraps of fabric
Plain cushion cover
Pins
Needle and thread
Iron

CHOOSING FABRICS

You can use any fabrics for the patches as long as they are a similar weight to the fabric of the cushion cover.

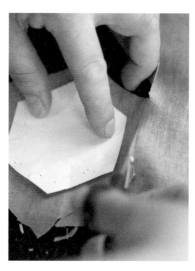

1 Trace the hexagon or diamond template on page 184 onto tracing paper, then cut it out of the card. Cut out six more hexagon shapes or five more diamond shapes in card. Using the card template as a guide, cut out a piece of fabric a little larger than the card shape—this does not need to be accurate, as the fabric will be held in the correct shape by the card. Make six more hexagon fabric shapes or five more diamond shapes.

2 Turn the edges of one of the fabric shapes over a card shape and pin in place. Baste (tack) the fabric to the card. Repeat with the remaining shapes.

Perfect partners: the gray of the Lloyd Loom chair is picked out exactly in the diamonds of the appliquéd cushion cover.

3 Holding the patch pieces right sides facing and making sure that the corners are aligned, whip stitch (oversew) together until you have a star pattern (if you are using diamonds) or a granny's garden pattern (if you are using hexagons). See the two finished cushions (left and on page 43) for reference. Leave the basting in the card for now.

4 Set the iron to the correct temperature for the fabrics you are using and press the pieced patches. This will keep the edges crisp and help the pieces to lay flat.

5 Carefully remove the basting stitches and the card from each of the patchwork shapes.

VARIATION

Adding a button to the center of the diamond pattern is a simple but effective finishing touch.

6 Pin the pieced shape to the center of the cushion cover and sew in place with slip stitch.

Graphic and eye-catching, hexagons, known as the granny's garden pattern (see far left) and diamonds, known as the star pattern (see above), are the most usual shapes found in English patchwork.

Denim windbreak

We've taken pairs of faded old jeans and turned them into this sturdy windbreak, which is the perfect accessory for picnics on the beach or camping in the country. You can make the windbreak as big as you like by simply adding more poles—here we've used just three. Denim is a strong, closely woven cloth, so you will need a sturdy needle in your sewing machine.

You will need

Old pairs of denim jeans
Ruler or tape measure
Tailor's chalk, pencil, or vanishing
marker pen
Scissors
Pins
Sewing machine
Lining fabric
Needle and strong thread
Webbing tape
6 large decorative buttons
(2 per pole)
3 wooden poles, such as broomsticks
Pencil
6 brass screw eyes (2 per pole)
Awl (bradawl)

Hardwearing denim is the ideal fabric for a windbreak. Keeping the detailing of embroidered pockets and seams adds to the rustic charm.

1 Measure, then cut your jeans into roughly equal-sized rectangles— we cut 45 rectangles measuring approximately 12 x 8in/30 x 20cm from ours, but the number all depends on the size of your jeans.

2 Piece them together by overlapping the long edges of the rectangles by approximately 1in/2.5cm and pin, to create the first strip. Our windbreak is made up of three long strips, each comprising 15 rectangles—see the finished project (opposite) for reference— but you can adjust the size to suit. Keep any frayed edges to add to the lived-in look.

3 Using a sewing machine, sew the pieces together, making one long strip. Make the second and third strips in the same way. Pin the three strips together, then machine-stitch.

4 Lay out your patchwork right side up—on the floor is easiest—and pin the lining fabric to it right side down. Stitch the two fabrics together along the four sides, leaving a gap about 10in/25cm wide halfway along one of the sides. Turn the whole piece right sides out through the gap, then slip stitch the gap closed.

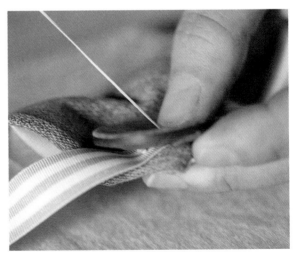

5 Cut the webbing tape into six 16-in/40-cm lengths to make the ties. Sew a tie onto each corner of the windbreak and onto the middle top and bottom with a strong thread, stitching through both layers of fabric several times.

6 Sew a decorative button over the tie stitches—we used coconut shell buttons.

7 Lay the windbreak on the floor, then put the poles in position. Mark the position of the screw eyes with a pencil, aligned with the top and bottom of the windbreak. At each mark, make a hole with an awl (bradawl), then screw in the screw eyes.

VARIATIONS

Decorative features such as embroidered pockets and seams, will give added interest to the windbreak.

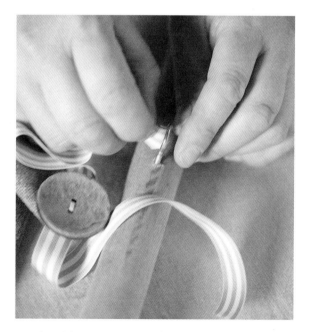

8 Thread the ties through the screw eyes, then tie the windbreak onto the poles.

Quilted deckchair cover

This lightly quilted seat pad is a great way to brighten up an old deckchair without having to replace the canvas, and it's also very comfortable. It is simple to make and a good way to introduce yourself to quilting and patchwork using a sewing machine. You will need to do a few calculations to get the size of the squares right for your chair, but it's worth taking the time to measure and cut accurately because doing so will make it easier to put the cover together.

You will need

Scraps of fabric, for the squares

Tape measure

Tailor's chalk, pencil, or vanishing marker pen

Scissors

Iron

Fabric, for the backing

Pins

Batting (wadding)

Sewing tape

Pompom trim (optional)

Needle and thread, if using a trim

Sewing machine

Ruler

1 Measure and mark out the fabric squares, remembering to include seam allowances—we measured 7in/18cm all around to end up with 6-in-/15-cm squares. Cut out.

MEASURING CORRECTLY

It is important to measure the deckchair sling so that you can work out the size of your patchwork squares. The sling of our chair is 18in/45cm wide and 42in/108cm long, so we used 21 x 6-in-/15-cm squares arranged in a rectangle of three squares across and seven squares down. Take note of where to place any ties that can be used to help keep the pad in place.

2 Piece the squares together in strips, as described in the Knitting bag project (see page 64). Press the seams open with an iron as you work.

3 When you have joined all the squares into one piece, lay it out on top of the backing fabric and use this as a guide for cutting out the backing fabric to size. Cut out the batting (wadding) to the same size as both the front and back fabrics.

4 Cut the sewing tape to length for the ties, so that they are long enough to tie to the frame of the chair. We used a piece of tape measuring 20in/50cm folded in half to make two ties for each of the four corners of our chair cover.

TAKE CARE

Before you start sewing your patchwork pieces together, experiment with different color and pattern combinations.

5 Put the front and back pieces of the cover together, right sides facing. Place the wadding beneath the two layers of fabric and pin the three layers together. If you would like to use a trim, such as a pompom, pin and baste (tack) it onto the right side of the patchwork piece before pinning the layers together.

6 Pin the ties in place as shown, between the front and back fabrics, with the long ends on the inside.

7 Machine-stitch around all four sides through all the layers, leaving a gap of approximately 10in/25cm. Turn the cover the right way out through the gap. Make sure that you push the corners out—use something blunt like the wrong end of a pencil—and that all the fabric is sitting flat. Tuck in the edges of the fabric at the gap, making sure that everything lines up, then pin together.

8 Topstitch the two long sides of the pad with the sewing machine, to help keep the edges crisp, and close the gap that was left after turning out the cover. Try to get the stitch line as close to the edge as you can.

9 Using the ruler, mark with tailor's chalk where you would like the quilting lines to go. Pin along these lines, to help keep all the layers together, then machine-stitch. We chose to quilt diagonally across the cover but you can also quilt along the lines where the squares are joined. Once completed, tie the cover to the chair over the canvas.

Patchwork beanbag

Patchwork shapes—diamonds and hexagons—are the inspiration behind this fun, hexagon-shaped beanbag. See the templates on page 184 to see how these two shapes fit together to form the hexagon pattern. We've made this project from scraps of fabric that would otherwise have been thrown away. Old furnishing fabrics, which have aged and faded gloriously, have been used for the top, while an old towel has been used for part of the bottom. All the fabrics are washable, which makes the beanbag very practical for outdoor use.

1 Using the paper template as a guide, cut out six diamonds from the calico, adding a ½-in/1-cm seam allowance. Join three of the diamonds together, using the diagram with the templates as a guide, to make up the hexagon pattern. The measurement from the center of the pattern to the edge should be 18in/45cm.

2 Pin the remaining single calico diamonds to each of the three fabrics that form the top of the beanbag. Cut out around the calico shape to create matching diamonds.

You will need

Diamond template (see page 184),
enlarged so the sides measure
18in/45cm

Tailor's chalk, pencil, or vanishing
marker pen

Ruler

Scissors

Pins

80 x 50in/203 x 127cm of calico or
an old sheet, for the hexagon pattern

Sewing machine

3 pieces of different fabric for the
top, each measuring at least
34 x 20in/86 x 50cm

3 pieces of matching fabric for the
sides, each measuring
40 x 5in/102 x 13cm

Fabric measuring at least
32 x 16in/81 x 40.5cm, for the
bottom of the beanbag

Piece of old towel measuring at least
26 x 36in/66 x 91cm, for the bottom
of the beanbag

Piece of fabric for the button loop

Large button or Velcro

Needle and thread

A removable and washable cover makes
this comfortable patchwork beanbag ideal
for using outdoors.

3 Using your calico hexagon pattern as a guide, pin the fabric diamonds for the top of the beanbag together with right sides facing and the pins at right angles to the line that the stitching will follow. Pinning in this way means that the presser foot on your sewing machine will ride right over the pins and the needle will not hit them. Machine-stitch together, taking a ½-in/1-cm seam allowance. If you're nervous about doing this, pin in the usual way, parallel to the line of sewing, then baste (tack) the fabrics together before sewing.

4 Using the hexagon pattern as a guide, cut the fabric for the bottom so that it will cover half of the underside of the beanbag and machine stitch the longest edge with a double ½-in/1-cm hem. This forms one half of the envelope opening, the edge of the old towel forms the other. Make sure that the towelling part will overlap the fabric part by 4in/10cm before cutting it, using the hexagon pattern as a guide.

5 Machine-stitch together the pieces of fabric for the sides of the beanbag, to make a long strip measuring 109 x 5in/ 277 x 13cm. Pin and machine-stitch the strip to the pieced beanbag top, taking care to include the seam allowance. Repeat to attach the two pieces cut in step 4, that form the bottom of the beanbag.

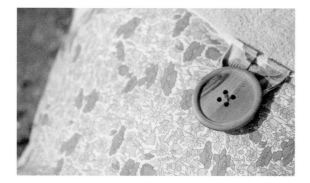

6 Turn the cover right sides out through the envelope opening made by the two overlapping fabrics on the bottom of the beanbag. For the fastening, you could use a sew-on touch-and-close fastener, such as Velcro, or a large button, as we have here. To make the button loop, cut out a piece of fabric measuring 8 x 6in/20 x 15cm and fold it in half lengthwise. Fold it in half again so that you have four layers of fabric, and the strip measures 8 x 1½in/20 x 4cm. Machine-stitch along both long sides of the loop, then sew the short ends firmly onto the beanbag. Sew on the button—we used a thread in a contrasting color.

BEANBAG LINER
To make the beanbag liner, cut out two hexagons from an old sheet, 2in/5cm larger all around than your calico pattern, and also cut out a strip measuring 6 x 121in/15 x 307cm, for the sides. Sew these pieces together in the same manner as the cover (see step 5), leaving an opening through which you can pour polystyrene beans. Keep pouring until the beanbag is as plump as you would like, then machine-stitch the opening closed. Insert the filler through the envelope opening of the cover. Plump the beanbag, then fasten the button.

Knitting bag

We mixed bright linens and faded floral fabrics with knitting-bag handles for a great vintage look. Pieced together from squares, this bag is quick to make because almost all the stitching is done on the sewing machine. Accurate measuring is the key to a successful result, so don't rush this stage or you will run into trouble when trying to match up your squares! You can adapt this pattern to fit different-sized handles—just do a few calculations first, and remember to include seam allowances. We've allowed seam allowances of ½in/1cm throughout this project.

You will need

Tailor's chalk, pencil, or vanishing marker pen

Ruler

1 yard/1 m (in total) fabric in different colors

1 yard/1 m lining fabric

Scissors

Pins

Sewing machine

Iron

Pair of knitting-bag handles—ours measure 7½ x 5½in/19 x 14cm

1 Mark out seven 5-in/13-cm squares in each of the four fabrics, to give you 28 squares. Cut out. Each cut-out square includes a seam allowance of ½in/1cm. When sewn together, they will be 4-in/10-cm squares.

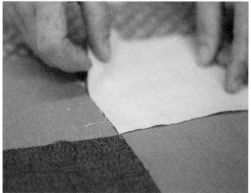

2 Lay out the squares and shuffle them around to see how well the different colors and fabrics work together.

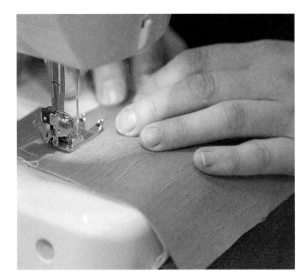

3 Pin and then machine-stitch the squares together in rows, using the measurement guide on your sewing machine to keep the stitching line straight. Press the seams open at each stage with an iron set at the correct temperature for the fabrics that you are using.

4 Continue to piece the squares together until they look like the photograph—the four squares in the center will form the base of the bag. Lay out the lining fabric, then lay the patchwork on top. Pin together. Cut the lining to the same shape and size as the patchwork. Remove the pins and keep the lining separate.

5 Fold the patchwork in half horizontally along the center of the four squares that form the base, so that the right sides are facing. Pin the sides together, matching the seams, and machine-stitch. You should have a bag with two holes in the bottom corners. Do the same with the lining fabric.

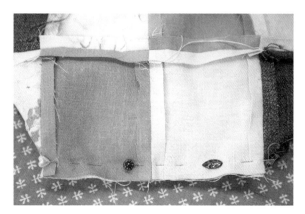

6 Pin the corners as shown, then stitch together. The bag should now have the four squares as the base and will still be inside out, with the seams on the outside of the bag. Pin and stitch the lining in the same way and then turn that right side out so that the seams are inside the bag.

7 Fit the bag exterior and the lining together, right sides facing, making sure that the corners match up. Pin the sides together. Working from the lining side, mark 2in/5cm either side of the joining seam with pins. Machine-stitch between these pins, using the reverse setting on the machine at the start and finish. This forms the sides of the bag that are each side of the bag handles.

8 Turn the bag right sides out so that the patchwork is outside and the lining inside. You should be able to see the unfinished edges of fabric, which is where the handles are to be sewn.

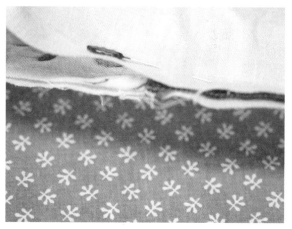

9 Cut out four pieces of lining fabric measuring 13 x 4in/ 33 x 10cm—these will form the sections that join the bag handles to the bag. Pin them together, right sides facing, and machine-stitch the short ends together, as shown, before turning them right sides out. Press flat.

10 Pin and then stitch the bag handle flap to the bag along the raw edges of the fabric between the sewn edges that form the sides of the bag.

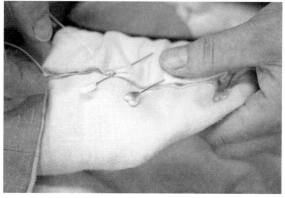

12 Sew the handle flap onto the bag lining with either whip stitch (oversew) or slip stitch.

11 Push the handle flap fabric through the slot in the handle and pin in place, tucking in the seam allowance and pinning along the stitch line that you can see on the inside of the bag. This will cover all the raw edges and neaten the inside of the bag.

TAKE CARE

Take your time when sewing a number of layers of fabric together. Basting (tacking) the layers together first could save you a lot of grief!

Chapter Three
Creative Candles

Atmospheric, aromatic, and useful, candles have perhaps never been more popular in the home than they are today. Of course, it is possible to buy them premade but that can work out to be very expensive. Instead, why not use the beautiful ideas in this chapter to spark your creativity and make your own candles?

Starting with a basic soy wax candle recipe, we show you how to use pretty vintage glassware and terra-cotta pots as containers, and even make your own firelighters. Take pleasure in using eco-friendly supplies to create inexpensive yet gorgeous candles for your home, as well as unique and personalized gifts that you will be proud to give.

Soy wax candles

Making your own candles with this soy wax-based recipe is a great eco-friendly alternative to using petroleum-derived wax. Soy wax has so many advantages, not least that it is a natural product made from a sustainable resource. It is also very easy to work with and has a lower burn temperature, which means increased "burn time" from each of your candles.

You need only the very minimum of equipment to make these candles, and the ingredients are readily available (see pages 188–9). Using this soy wax recipe as a base, you can then go on to create all sorts of different candles for yourself or as gifts. In this chapter, we show you how, as well as giving you lots of inspirational ideas. Before you start, make sure you read the section on safety on page 73.

FINISHING TOUCH

Adding candle fragrance oils to your candles will make them even more unique. These oils are available in a variety of fragrances, so you can combine different ones to create your own individual scents. Adding citronella to an outdoor candle will help to keep the bugs at bay. Always use oils that are suitable for candle-making.

You will need

Soy wax flakes (3½oz/100g of candle
wax melts down to about 6fl oz,
just under 200ml, enough to
fill approximately two small teacup-
size containers)
Length of unwaxed candle wick (see
box, below, for guidance)
Candle fragrance oil (optional; make
sure you use fragrance oil that is
suitable for candle-making)

Equipment
Double boiler (bain-marie)
Large Pyrex or heatproof glass
pitcher (jug)
Cooking thermometer
Stirring utensil, such as a
wooden stick
Heat-resistant gloves
Scissors
Candle container

1 Set up the double boiler (bain-
marie)—we used a large, old
saucepan and placed a metal ring in
the bottom. Add water so that the pan
is about one-third full.

2 Place a large Pyrex pitcher (jug) or
other heatproof container on top
of the metal ring so that it doesn't touch
the heat source. Bring your water to
simmering point, then scoop the soy wax
flakes into the pitcher.

BUYING WICKS

*Most suppliers use their own sizing system for wicks, so follow your
supplier's advice as to what size you need to buy. The fragrance you
add, the type of container, and, of course, the size of the candle all have
a bearing on the size of wick you need. It is really a case of experimenting.
Following our supplier's guide (Gentil Sayre—see pages 188–9), we have
used Eco 1 unwaxed wicks for all our projects because the containers
are relatively small. Once you have experimented a few times and seen the
burn pool created by the candles once they are lit, it will be easier to judge
whether you need to use a thicker or thinner wick.*

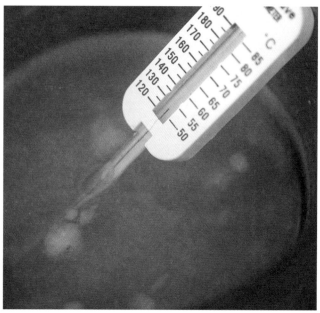

3 Stir the soy flakes from time to time to agitate—there is no need to stir them constantly.

4 Once the flakes have dissolved—this doesn't take long but the time does vary according to the amount of flakes used—check the temperature with a cooking thermometer. It should be between 130° and 135° F/54° and 57° C.

5 Remove the pitcher carefully from the double boiler using heat-resistant gloves. Turn off the heat. Allow the wax to cool a little before pouring into your chosen container—see the other projects in this chapter.

MAKING WAXED WICKS

You can buy ready-waxed candle wicks but it is preferable to use wicks that have been covered in the same type of wax that you are using for your candle. Making your own is so easy as part of the wax-melting process that it seems pointless to buy them. Simply dip the cut wick into the melted wax, remove it, straighten, and let harden for a few seconds (see step 6).

6 Cut a length of unwaxed wick and dip it into the melted wax. Set to one side to harden, keeping the wick straight. This gives the wick more strength when it is placed in the container and makes it stay straight.

7 To make a fragrant candle, add fragrance to the wax. As a guide, it is recommended that you add between 5% and 12%. For example, 1oz (28g) of fragrance oil to 1lb (453g) of wax will result in a 6% concentration. Stir well to ensure the fragrance oil is thoroughly mixed into the melted wax.

Stay safe

As well as taking care when burning candles —never leave a burning candle unattended—you should also take great care when melting wax. It is potentially one of the most dangerous aspects of candle-making. Follow these safety precautions:

- Make sure your working environment is safe. Have everything you need within easy reach.
- Protect work surfaces adequately and be prepared to deal with any spillages. Have a fire extinguisher or blanket nearby, and also a lid or wet dishtowel to cover the wax melting pot should it ignite (do NOT use water!).
- Keep children and pets away from your working area and ensure that the handles of any pans are turned in and away from countertop edges.
- Handle fragrance oils with care. They are highly concentrated and can cause stains, as well irritation to the skin. Clear any spillages at once and wash your hands.
- Use an electric heat source, if possible, for heating the wax. This is because if, by accident, the wax reaches flashpoint, it is less likely that the vapors will become ignited on an electric heat source. The flashpoint for wax is typically above 300° F/149° C. Never let your wax exceed 250° F/121° C.
- Use a double boiler (bain-marie) system, with a thermometer in the wax at all times. A double boiler helps distribute heat and prevents dangerously high temperatures. Never melt wax directly in a pan on your stove.
- Never leave melting wax unattended. If you have to leave the room in the middle of melting the wax, move the double boiler away from the heat source first or extinguish the flame.

Glass preserving jar candle

Everyday containers can easily be turned into beautiful and inexpensive gifts. For this project, we've used a small glass preserving jar. You can personalize it in many different ways, such as with a favorite fragrance or vintage ribbons and trimmings. Once the candle has burned, clean the jar well and use it again!

You will need

Melted soy wax, fragranced or unscented, enough to almost fill the preserving jar (see pages 71–3)

Scissors

Waxed candle wick (see page 73)

Glue dot

Glass preserving jar

Bamboo skewer

Metal food twist tie

To decorate

Small luggage tag

Small strip of vintage lace

Double-sided tape

Button

Glue dot

Natural twine

1 Make the melted soy wax, following the steps on pages 71–3. Leave out step 7 if you want your candle to be unscented. Cut a length of waxed wick 4in/10cm or so longer than the height of the jar. Stick a glue dot to one end of the wick, then stick this to the middle of the bottom of the jar. This will keep the wick in place when you pour in the melted wax.

2 Wrap the other end of the waxed wick around the middle of the bamboo skewer, securing with the twist tie. Place the skewer centrally across the top of the jar.

3 Place the jar on a heatproof surface and carefully pour the melted wax into the jar, leaving a gap of about 1in/2.5cm between the wax and the top of the jar. Move the jar to a safe, draft-free place for the wax to set and harden completely. The amount of time that this takes will depend on the room temperature and volume of wax. Ideally, allow 24 hours. Make sure that the wick remains in the middle of the jar, to ensure even burning when the candle is lit.

4 Once the wax has set, remove the skewer and cut the wick to about 1in/2.5cm from the top of the candle, then decorate the jar. Here, we used an old-fashioned luggage tag onto which we typed the words "With Love." Alternatively, use a rubber stamp or handwrite your message. Decorate the tag with a strip of vintage lace, securing it with double-sided tape, and an old button, fixed with a glue dot. Attach the tag to the jar with a length of natural twine or a ribbon in a favorite color.

PREPARING JARS

It is a good idea to make sure that your glass preserving jars are clean, dry, and dust-free before making these candles. Wash the jars in hot soapy water and dry them thoroughly before starting the project. This will ensure your candle looks as though it has been made by a professional!

A plain brown luggage tag decorated with a strip of ribbon, tied onto the clasp with rough string, is the perfect finishing touch to this beautiful candle gift.

Vintage sundae dish candle

Glassware comes in so many pretty decorative shapes and sizes that you will have no problem in locating lots of lovely containers to experiment with.

Hunt around at home and when you are out and about. We found these really delicate vintage sundae dishes at a local yard sale (car boot fair) and thought they were ideal for use as candle containers.

You will need

Melted soy wax, fragranced or unscented, enough to almost fill the sundae dish (see pages 71–3)

Scissors

Waxed candle wick (see page 73)

Glue dot

Glass sundae dish

Bamboo skewer

Metal food twist tie

Ribbon, to decorate

Pretty vintage ice-cream sundae dishes make gorgeous candle containers. There is no need for any embellishment, except, perhaps, for a discreet gingham ribbon tied around the neck in a bow.

1 Make the melted soy wax, following the steps on pages 71–3. Leave out step 7 if you want your candle to be unscented. Cut a length of waxed wick 4in/10cm longer than the height of the dish. Stick a glue dot to one end of the wick, then stick this to the middle of the bottom of the dish. This will keep the wick in place when you pour in the melted wax. (The picture to the left shows the wick being positioned in a glass preserving jar, not a sundae dish, but the method is the same.)

2 Wrap the other end of the waxed wick around the middle of the bamboo skewer, securing with the twist tie. Place the skewer centrally across the top of your sundae dish.

3 Place the dish on a heatproof surface and carefully pour in the melted soy wax, leaving a gap of about 1in/2.5cm between the wax and the top of the dish.

4 Let the candle set in a safe, draft-free place. Make sure the skewer remains centrally placed over the top of the dish, with the wick set in the middle of the candle, so that the candle burns evenly when lit. The room temperature and volume of wax will affect the amount of time it takes for the wax to harden completely. Ideally, allow 24 hours.

5 When the wax has set completely, remove the skewer and cut the wick to about 1in/2.5cm from the top of the candle. Add any embellishments you wish. As the dish itself is so pretty, we felt only a simple addition was needed, so we tied a bow of narrow, purple gingham ribbon around the neck of the dish.

VARIATIONS

Why not use pretty vintage teacups and saucers as candle containers? You could even create a whole tea-set using a combination of different but complementary patterns. Wrapped in gathered cellophane, tied with a ribbon bow, each cup and saucer would make a wonderful gift, as would the vintage glass sundae dishes.

USING GLASS CONTAINERS

When using vintage glassware as candle containers, make sure the glass is free from cracks or fractures before preparing for use. Also, allow the wax to cool a little before pouring into vintage glassware, to prevent it from breaking or cracking.

Terra-cotta candle pots

Terra-cotta pots come in an infinite number of shapes and sizes. You may even have some lurking in your back yard, but if not, they are easily obtainable. This project uses a small flowerpot and an oddment of vintage lace and old buttons for decoration, creating a really handsome candle that is attractive even when not lit! The possibilities for decoration are endless, so let your imagination run wild. The pots are wonderful to use indoors or out, and make perfect gifts.

You will need

Terra-cotta flowerpot
Sealant (50:50 mix of latex solution/PVA to water)
Paintbrush
Clear sealant
Water-based paint
Melted soy wax, fragranced or unscented, enough to almost fill the terra-cotta pot (see pages 71–3)
Scissors
Waxed candle wick (see page 73)
Bamboo skewer
Metal food twist tie

To decorate
Vintage lace oddment
Double-sided tape
3 small decorative buttons
Glue dots

1 Seal the flowerpot inside and out using a 50:50 mix of latex solution to water, to prevent the unsealed terra-cotta from cracking when in use as a candle container. Seal the hole at the bottom of the pot with a blob of clear sealant. Leave for 24 hours to dry completely.

2 Paint the outside of the flowerpot with two coats of water-based paint—a sample paint pot is the perfect size for the task if you don't have any leftover paint you can use. Let the first coat dry before applying the second.

TAKE CARE

Always place candleholders on heat resistant surfaces to avoid heat damage.

3 Make the melted soy wax, following the steps on pages 71–3, leaving out step 7 if you want your candle to be unscented. Cut a length of waxed wick 4in/10cm longer than the height of the pot. Stick a glue dot to one end of the wick, then stick this to the middle of the bottom of the pot. This will keep the wick in place when you pour in the melted wax. Wrap the other end of the wick around the middle of the bamboo skewer, securing with the twist tie. Place the skewer centrally across the top of the pot.

4 Place the pot on a heatproof surface and carefully pour the melted soy wax into the pot. Do not fill right to the top but leave around ½in/1cm of clearance. Move the pot to a safe, draft-free place for the wax to set and harden completely. The amount of time that this takes will depend on the room temperature and volume of wax. Ideally, allow 24 hours. Make sure that the wick remains in the middle of the pot, to ensure even burning when the candle is lit.

Once the wax has set, remove the skewer and cut the wick to around ½in/1cm from the top of the candle. Fix a small piece of double-sided tape to each end of the lace and wrap around the top of the pot. Stick glue dots to each of the buttons and arrange in a vertical line on the pot.

VARIATIONS

For a more rustic look, leave the terra-cotta on show. Seal the hole in the same way and stencil just a small motif on the outside by way of decoration.

Illuminating your yard at night with a selection of terra-cotta candle pots creates a lovely ambience. Citronella in the wax gives off a subtle, lemony scent, which helps to deter flying bugs.

Pine cone firelighters

For a natural, more attractive alternative to chemical-based firelighters, and one that smells lovely too, look no further! Take yourself off for a walk with a purpose and collect some fallen pine cones for this project—what better excuse do you need? As well as being simple to make and very practical, these firelighters can also make a decorative addition to the fireplace before you use them.

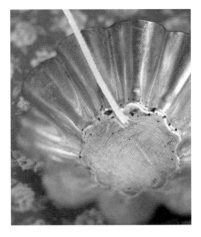

1 Make the melted soy wax, following the steps on pages 71–3. Leave out step 7 if you want your candle to be unscented. Lightly spray the molds with the candle-making oil so that the wax is easy to remove once it has set. Cut lengths of waxed wick about 1–1½in/4cm longer than the height of the molds. Place a wick in each one.

2 Place the prepared molds onto a heat-resistant surface, then carefully pour the melted wax into the molds, leaving a small gap at the top.

You will need

Melted soy wax, fragranced or unscented, enough to almost fill the molds (see pages 71–3)
Metal molds or containers for the base, such as vintage metal patisserie pans or old muffin pans
Olive oil spray
Waxed candle wick (see page 73)
Scissors
Pine cones, thoroughly dried out so they burn more efficiently

VARIATIONS

To fragrance the candle wax for these firelighters, try adding cinnamon, a perennial winter favorite. Alternatively, use orange, pine, or eucalyptus.

3 Put the filled molds aside to set slightly. Before the wax turns opaque, gently place the pine cones in the melted wax.

4 Let the wax harden and set completely. Although it will depend on the size of the molds, this should not take more than a couple of hours, but you may prefer to wait overnight to be sure.

5 Bend the molds slightly to gently release the wax. The firelighters are now ready to use or to wrap as a gift. To use, place one firelighter among kindling in the fireplace, and light the wick.

GIFT WRAPPING

These firelighters would make a delightful, and very personal, housewarming or winter dinner party gift. Simply gather a few together, wrap them in clear cellophane or a piece of burlap (hessian), and tie with a gingham ribbon bow and a gift tag.

Beeswax candles

These candles are incredibly easy and fun to make. They're really eco-friendly, too, because they're made from beeswax, which comes in sheets ready to use, and each sheet makes two candles. We bought our sheets from a local craft store but if yours doesn't stock them, they are available on the internet (see pages 188–9)

You will need

Beeswax sheets
Ruler
Sharp knife
Waxed candle wick (see page 73)
Scissors

To decorate
Brown paper
Burlap (hessian), frayed at the edges
Garden twine

PLACING THE WICK

When placing the wick in position on the beeswax sheet (see step 3), keep the wick ½in/1cm or so away from the bottom edge. This stops the candle burning right down to the base of the beeswax, so it burns out before reaching the last part of the wick.

1 Score a line diagonally through a sheet of beeswax using the ruler and knife.

2 Lift the two sides of the sheet—it should break easily into two pieces. Each half will make one candle.

3 Take one half of the sheet of beeswax and measure off a piece of waxed wick about 1in/2.5cm longer than the longest edge of the sheet. Place the wick lengthwise along this longest edge.

4 Roll the beeswax sheet carefully with your hands, rather like you would roll modeling clay. The beeswax is quite malleable and will respond to the warmth of your hands. Roll quite tightly to begin with, to make sure the wick is held securely inside the sheet.

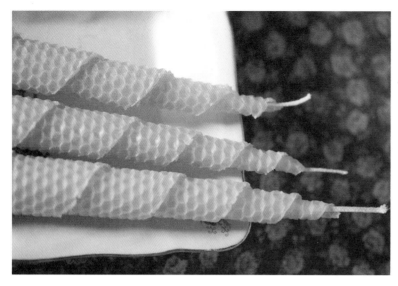

5 Continue to roll the sheet carefully and evenly until you have a candle with a spiral design.

6 Cut the wick to the desired length. Repeat the above steps with the second half of the beeswax sheet.

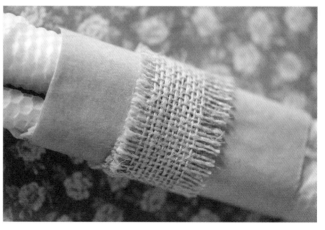

8 Wrap a strip of brown paper around a pair of beeswax candles, with the burlap centered over it.

7 To make the candles suitable for gift-giving, decorate them with a strip of brown paper, a small piece of burlap (hessian), and some garden twine.

9 Take a doubled length of twine and tie around the brown paper and burlap to secure the candles.

The simplest decoration is often the best. Brown paper, a strip of burlap (hessian), and contrasting garden twine are all that you need to turn these beeswax candles into a delightful gift.

Chapter Four

Weaving

This chapter covers the traditional country crafts of weaving and making rag rugs. Neither involves expensive equipment—we've even turned corrugated paper (cardboard) into a simple loom for weaving the basket on page 104. Both techniques can be used to make some really beautiful textiles for your home.

The humble rag rug is now a respected art form and they can be very expensive to buy—this is a reflection of the skill and time involved in creating a rug. This both amuses and delights people who can remember a time when almost every home would have them and whole families would take a part in the production of a rug. There are many stories of families who have existed on the income generated by rag rug making during very hard times. Try your hand at this old craft for pleasure rather than necessity— making rag rugs is a great way of recycling textiles and very satisfying.

Basic techniques

For both weaving and making rag rugs, do start to experiment with techniques and fabrics once you have mastered the basics. You will find a lot of information about both crafts on the internet, including instructions and tutorials. We've listed some useful web addresses on pages 188–9).The equipment list for rag rug making is a short one—hessian, rags, and a hook or proddy—that's it! You do, however, need the right sort of hook or proddy: the handle should be short and rounded so that it sits comfortably in your hand; this will make forcing the rags through the hessian much easier and kinder to your hands.

Weaving

Weaving simply involves passing one fiber called the weft, over and under another one called the warp. Weights, pegs, and frames are all used to hold the warps tight during weaving and you don't need expensive equipment to create some textiles for use in your home.

The weft can be made up of yarns (wool), fleece, and even rags to create rag rugs. Use a variety of materials together to great effect: the little cushion with the button detail shown left is made by weaving rags, fleece, and yarns through some linen twine. The rags fray a little but this just adds texture and interest to the finished cushion. Experiment with some unusual materials and you may be pleasantly surprised at the fabric you produce at the end.

Peg loom weaving is a very old technique and means that you need very little room to work, but can still create large rugs quite quickly. Peg looms are inexpensive to buy and are quite easily made by someone with a little woodworking experience. There are a lot of instructions and tutorials on the internet.

Rag rugs

Rag rugs have long played a part in thrifty homemaking, using scraps of fabrics and weaving, braiding (plaiting), or attaching them to a backing with hand tools. In some cases even the backing would have been recycled from an old sack! Amongst the pictures within this chapter are some rugs made by Lisa Linsdell, who uses aerial views of landscapes as inspiration. However, do not feel pressured to follow a pattern, as rugs worked randomly can also look spectacular.

It's worth taking a bit of time to experiment with a variety of fabrics and techniques to see which ones will work best with your design. Lisa favors old T-shirts for her hooked rugs, as by the time that they have lost their shape and are no longer wearable the repeated washing that they have been subjected to softens the fabric and gently fades

the colors. The techniques of rag rug making are not just for rugs and can also be used to great effect on bags, cushions, and wall hangings. The most commonly seen techniques are hooking, prodding, braiding, and weaving.

A TRADITIONAL CRAFT

Rag rug making is not a hobby for anyone who likes a speedy project as it is a time-consuming pastime. Traditionally, people would settle down to make them in front of the fire on a chilly winter's evening and many older people I've spoken to can remember cutting up old clothes into strips in preparation for hooking or prodding.

Making and using a frame loom

Making a weaving loom yourself couldn't be simpler. All you need is lengths of
1 x 1in/25 x 25mm lumber (timber), a staple gun, and a hammer and nails. The
nails are used for wrapping the long warp threads around, to keep them tight while
you are weaving, and it also enables you to work your weaving from both sides.
Here, we've used a linen twine for the warp threads, and linen rags for the filling
(weft). The size of the finished piece depends on the frame—this size of frame
would be ideal for weaving a cushion cover.

You will need

2 sections of 1 x 1in/25 x 25mm
lumber (timber), each measuring
31in/79cm
2 sections of 1 x 1in/25 x 25mm
lumber (timber), each measuring
20in/50cm
Staple gun
Pencil
Ruler
Hammer
Nails
Linen twine, for the warp thread
Scissors
Rags cut into strips 2–4in/5–10cm
wide, to form the filling (weft)

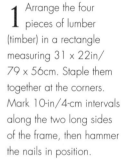

1 Arrange the four pieces of lumber (timber) in a rectangle measuring 31 x 22in/ 79 x 56cm. Staple them together at the corners. Mark 10-in/4-cm intervals along the two long sides of the frame, then hammer the nails in position.

2 Starting in one corner, tie the linen twine to the first nail with a knot.

4 Still holding the twine, pass it around the next nail along and then across the frame to the nail opposite. Continue to do this until all the warp threads are in place, then tie a knot around the last nail to secure the warp, ensuring that the twine is held tightly. Cut the twine.

3 Pull the twine over to the nail on the opposite side of the frame and pass the twine around that nail. Take the twine back across the frame to the first nail that you tied the twine to at the beginning.

6 Continue to weave in this way, and each time you come to the end of a strip, overlap it with the next by about 4in/10cm. Make sure that you push the filling tightly up against the previous row as you go.

5 Holding the loom so that the warp threads are vertical and you are working from right to left (or left to right, if you are left-handed), pass the filling (weft) material over and under each warp thread. Working back in the other direction, pass the filling over and under the warp again but this time making sure that the filling passes over a warp that had previously been passed under.

FINISHING TOUCH

To finish and remove the fabric from the loom, cut each warp thread with scissors as close to the nail as you can get. Tie the warp threads together in pairs and knot firmly. You can leave the ends long to form a tasseled fringe or sew them into the edge of the weaving before trimming them.

Weaving with a peg loom

As the name suggests, peg loom weaving is done on short wooden pegs, which measure about 4in/10cm, held in a frame. The warps are threaded through the pegs in such a way that when the pegs are full of weaving, they are removed from the frame and the woven section is slid down the warps before the pegs are replaced in readiness for the next section of weaving.

Even though peg looms take up very little room, you can still weave large pieces of fabric and even make rugs with them. They are great for using with yarns (wool), rags, and fleece, and children particularly enjoy weaving with them. For our basket, we've used undyed fleece from Wensleydale sheep, which is curly, soft, and a lovely color, combined with fleece that we dyed with woad (see page 143). You can, however, use just one type of fleece and adapt the steps below accordingly.

1 Cut the linen twine into 45 lengths, each measuring 30in/76cm, to make the warps for the sides of the basket. Thread a length of twine through the small hole at the base of each peg.

2 Place the threaded pegs in the frame, with the threaded hole closest to the frame. Make sure that the warp threads are even, then knot the threads from each pair of pegs together firmly. Each knot should be made up of four strands of warp thread.

You will need

Linen twine, for the warp thread

Scissors

Peg loom, measuring 35in/89cm, with 45 pegs

1lb/454g of fleece (in total), dyed and undyed

Tape measure

Pins

Needle and thread

Large wooden button, to finish

3 Start to weave pieces of fleece in and out of the pegs. Build up the weaving by alternating which way you lay the fleece around the pegs and overlapping when you join in a new piece of fleece.

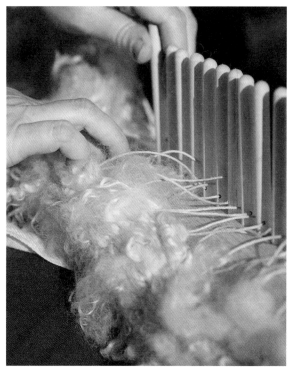

4 When the pegs are full of fleece, move on to the next section by pulling out all of the pegs and bringing with them some of the warp thread.

5 Replace the pegs in the frame, taking care to keep the threads straight and to put the pegs back into their original holes. Continue weaving as before. Halfway up the pegs, we changed to woad-dyed fleece but you can continue with the same fleece. Cast off the weaving by pulling out the pegs in pairs and cutting the warp threads.

6 Working along the loom, tie the warp threads together in pairs, pushing the weaving together tightly and knotting firmly.

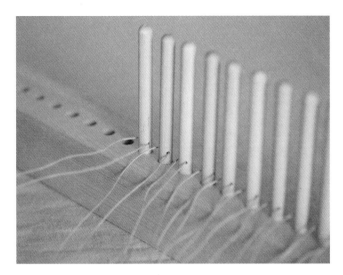

7 The base of the basket is made in the same way but you need thread only 12 of the pegs. Cut the warp threads at 40in/102cm and weave with the fleece until the work measures 9 x 8in/23 x 20cm. Cast off the weaving as in steps 5 and 6.

8 Assemble the basket by pinning the sides to the base so that the join on the sides of the basket overlaps a little. Sew on the wooden button to the basket at the overlapped point. Secure the base to the sides with some stitches—the curly fleece will hide them.

A simple square basket made by weaving a fleece weft with a linen twine warp, finished with a large wooden button.

Woven basket

This sweet little basket, woven in two different types of yarn, has been made using a frame loom for the sides of the basket, and a simple circular loom of corrugated paper (cardboard) for the bottom. The handspun chunky yarn on the sides, which gives a gorgeous, uneven look, is by Knit Collage (see pages 188–9). During the spinning process, tiny ribbon roses are added, along with neon-colored shoelaces, pieces of ribbon, and even some sparkly tinsel! The bottom of the basket is made with undyed chunky yarn spun from the fleece of Bluefaced Leicester sheep. These special yarns aren't crucial for the project but any alternatives need to be chunky.

You will need

Weaving frame (see page 98)
4oz/113g cotton string
5oz or 35 yards/142g or 32m chunky yarn, for the basket sides
Scissors
Corrugated paper (cardboard)
4oz or 20 yards/113g or 18m Bluefaced Leicester chunky yarn, or similar, for the basket bottom
Needle and strong thread

1 Make and set the warp threads on your weaving frame following the instructions on pages 98–9, using cotton string instead of linen twine. Weave the chunky yarn for the sides of the basket, following the instructions on page 99 for the rag strips. Continue weaving until the work measures approximately 18 x 8in/ 45 x 20cm.

2 Tie off the ends of all the warp threads, knotting them together firmly in pairs, and trim. Put to one side while you weave the bottom of the basket.

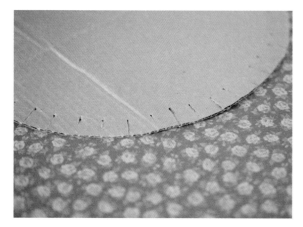

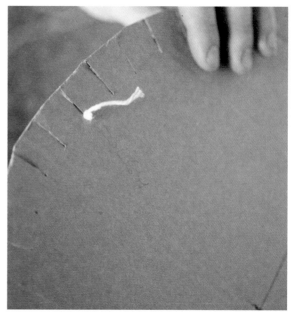

3 Cut out a circle of corrugated paper (cardboard) measuring 14in/35cm in diameter. Cut 1-in/2.5-cm slots at 1½-in/4-cm intervals all around the edge of the circle. Make sure there are an even number of slots.

4 Tie a knot in one end of the cotton string and tuck it into one of the slots on the corrugated paper circle, to secure.

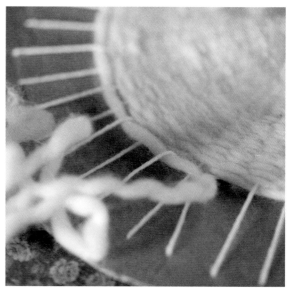

5 Locate the slot immediately opposite your starting point and bring the string over to it. Pass the string to the back of the circle over to the next slot and then bring it back to the front through the neighboring slot.

6 Using the Bluefaced Leicester yarn and starting in the center of the circle, weave over and under the warps, spiraling outward until the circle of weaving measures approximately 6in/15cm in diameter.

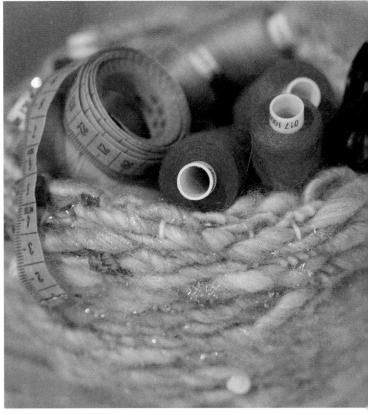

7 Cut the warps and tie them together in pairs. Knot securely and then trim.

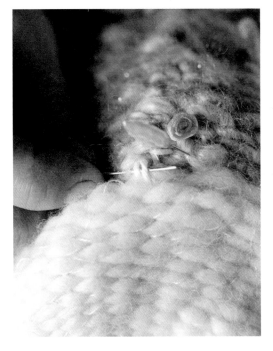

VARIATION

Instead of starting off with decorative yarn, why not embellish a plain yarn with buttons, beads, and ribbon roses after you've made up the basket?

8 Holding the square piece of weaving so that the warps are vertical, curve the fabric around so that it forms a tube. Slip stitch the edges together, then stitch the tube to the base, tucking in any ends as you go. Turn the top edge of the open end back on itself, like a shirt cuff, so that the "walls" of the basket stand up.

Twill tape cushion cover

Although not a weaving project, this smart cushion with interlaced herringbone twill tapes was inspired by weaving. The tapes are woven in and out of one another and attached within the side seams of the cushion cover. We've used a soft needlecord for the main fabric, and twill tapes in various colors and widths, to great decorative effect. Our finished cushion is 18 x 18in/45 x 45cm, and the measurements given below are for a cushion that size, with a 1-in/2.5-cm seam allowance. To ensure a good fit, make sure that your cushion form (pad) is 1in/2.5cm larger than your finished cushion.

You will need

Fabric, for the front and back of the cushion cover

Scissors

Herringbone twill tape in 3 different colors

Ruler

Pins

Sewing machine

Pencil

Feather cushion form (pad), measuring 17 x 17in/43 x 43cm

Inspired by weaving, interlaced twill ribbons have turned a plain cushion into a striking and sophisticated decorative feature.

1 Cut out two squares of fabric, each measuring 19 x 19in/ 48 x 48cm, for the front and back of the cushion cover. Decide how you wish the opening to be finished—we used a button closure but it could also be a zipper or an envelope-style opening. Whichever you choose, the opening must go across the back of the cushion. Cut two 19-in/ 48-cm lengths of twill tape in each color, making six lengths in total.

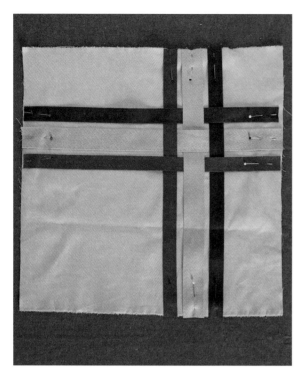

2 Position the tapes on the square of fabric for the front of the cushion cover, as shown in the photograph, measuring between the tapes with a ruler to ensure that they are set straight and that the spaces between them are even. We set the blue tape 4in/10cm in from the edge and left a space of ½in/1cm between that and the beige tape, and ½in/1cm between the beige and the red tape.

3 Pin the tapes to the cover as shown. This will eliminate the need to baste (tack) the tapes into place because the sewing-machine foot will ride over the pins and the needle will miss them. Machine-stitch the tapes on to the cover at the ends, along the seams.

TAKE CARE

To help the corners of your cushion cover sit flat, remove some of the excess fabric after machining the sides by snipping across the corners, but make sure that you cut no closer than ¼in/5mm to the stitch line.

4 Place the fabric for the back onto the decorated front, right sides facing, overlapping the two back pieces if making a button or envelope closure or inserting a zipper into the seam if using one back piece. Pin, then machine-stitch around all four sides, taking a seam allowance of 1in/2.5cm. Use the guide on your sewing machine to sew in a straight line. Turn the cover right sides out and use the blunt end of a pencil to help push out the corners. Insert the cushion form (pad).

Preparing the burlap backing

Both hooked and prodded rugs need to be worked onto a piece of burlap (hessian), which is stretched across a frame. This will serve as the rug backing. Here we show you how to fix the burlap to a square frame made from four pieces of 1 x 1in/25 x 25mm lumber (timber), each 18in/45cm long and stapled at each corner. For a large rug, when you have finished working the area within the frame and need to move on to the next section, take out the staples, reposition the burlap over the frame, and re-staple to hold in place. Alternatively, you can use a large embroidery hoop or a tapestry frame. The advantage of these is that no stapling is required. When you have finished the hooking or prodding, sew the burlap to the back of the rug for a neat edge.

You will need

Burlap (hessian), at least 8in/20cm
bigger all around than the piece
you are making
Scissors
Needle and thread or
sewing machine
Staple gun

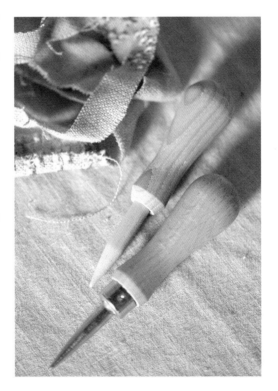

1 Fold over about 2in/5cm of the burlap (hessian) on all four sides. Stitch in place with a sewing machine, or sew by hand. The hemming prevents the burlap from fraying while you are hooking or prodding.

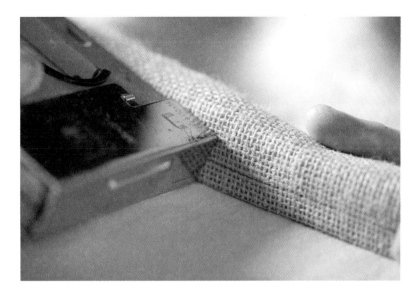

2 Staple the hemmed burlap to the frame along one side.

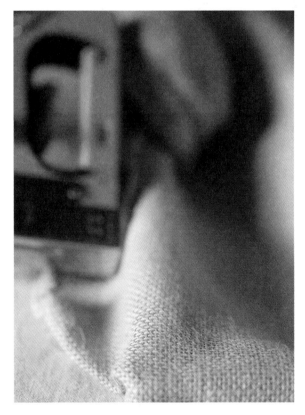

3 Stretch the burlap over the frame quite tightly and staple onto the opposite side of the frame.

4 Repeat until the burlap is fixed to all four sides of the frame, ensuring that it is pulled taut.

Hooked rag rug

Hooked rag rugs are made up of lots and lots of rag loops worked on burlap (hessian), which is stretched across a frame. Old T-shirts are great for this technique because they give a little as they are worked through the burlap, which helps the loops to stay firmly in place. Rugs made with strips from old denim jeans are firm and hardwearing, with all the different blues producing interesting shading. Putting different pieces of rag together before you start to make your rug will make it easier to decide which ones to use.

You will need

Burlap (hessian) 8in/20cm larger
all around than the rug you
wish to make
Frame, such as an embroidery hoop,
to hold the burlap tight
Rags
Scissors
Rag rug hook
Needle and strong thread

1 Fix the burlap (hessian) to the frame (see page 112). Cut the rags into strips about ½–1in/1–2.5cm wide (the strips can be any length that is workable); thin fabrics need to be cut into wider strips, thick fabrics into narrower strips.

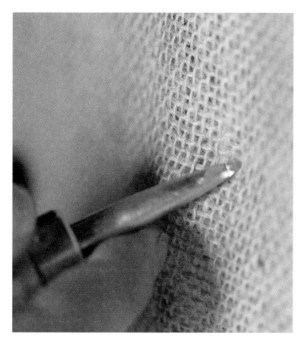

3 Wrap a rag strip around the hook, which is poking through
the back of the burlap.

2 Push the rag rug hook through the front of the burlap to the
back. You can start anywhere on the frame for a random
design, or mark a pattern onto the burlap.

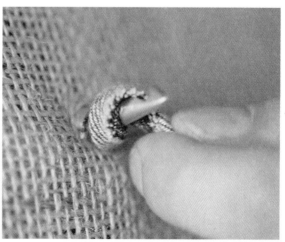

4 Pull the hook, and with it the rag, to the front of the burlap.
As this is the start of the hooking, leave about ½in/1cm of
the end of the rag sticking out through the front of the burlap, to
stop the hooking from unraveling.

5 Push the hook back through the burlap, close to the point
at which you started. Wrap the fabric around the hook, as
you did in step 3.

6 Pull the fabric back through the burlap but this time form a loop.

7 Continue in this way until the strip is used up. Pull the free end of fabric through to the front of the burlap to finish, before starting with the next piece. Keep hooking until all the burlap has been worked, right up to 2in/5cm from all the edges. To finish the rug at the edges, fold the burlap to the back of the rug and stitch into place with some strong thread.

FINISHING TOUCH

Cutting across the loops with large scissors creates an attractive pile on the rug surface and makes it comfortable underfoot.

Prodded rag rug

Rag rugs made by prodding have a shaggy appearance and are softer underfoot than their hooked counterparts. Worked from the back of the rug, they are made with short lengths of rag that are pushed through the burlap (hessian) with a proddy, which is simply a dowel pointed at one end, set in a handle. As with the hooked rag rugs, the burlap is held tight over a frame.

You will need

Burlap (hessian), 8in/20cm larger
all around than the prodded rag rug
you wish to make
Frame, such as an embroidery hoop,
to hold the burlap tight
Rags
Scissors
Proddy
Needle and strong thread

When all the burlap has been covered, these prodded denim scraps will turn into a shaggy-looking rag rug.

FINISHING TOUCH

When you finish the rug, you can paint the back of it with a diluted liquid latex solution. This will help to make it firmer and keep the rags in place.

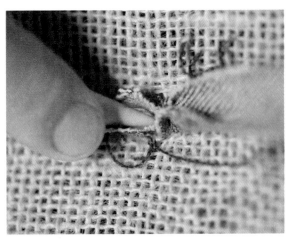

1 Fix the burlap (hessian) to the frame (see page 112). Cut the rags into strips about ½in–1in/1–2.5cm wide, then cut into 3-in/8-cm lengths.

2 Working from the back of the burlap, push one end of a strip of rag through the burlap using the proddy.

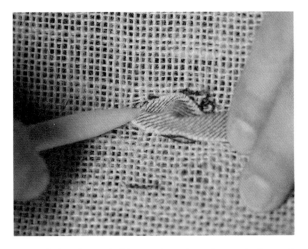

3 Push the other end of the rag through as close to the first end as you can get.

4 The back of the rug will look like this. Continue to prod the rug with rag strips up to 2in/5cm away from the edges of the burlap. Finish the rug edges by folding them to the back of the rug and stitching them into place with strong thread.

Decorative hooked flower motif

Using the rag rug hooking technique, we added a flower motif to a plain linen bag, but any unlined bag made of a loose-weave fabric would do. There is a flower template provided on page 185 but, if you prefer, you can always draw your own design freehand straight onto the fabric, as shown.

You will need

Pencil

Paper

Flower template (see page 185)

Tailor's chalk, pencil, or vanishing marker pen

Transfer paper

Plain loose-weave bag, unlined

Embroidery hoop

Scissors

Rags

Rag rug hook

KEEP IT SIMPLE

When creating your design, remember that clean lines and simple shapes are not only easier to work but can also be much more effective. Less really is more! Take a look at traditional folk art for inspiration.

1 Draw your chosen design on paper, then transfer the design onto the bag with transfer paper, or draw the design freehand straight onto the fabric. Alternatively, transfer the template from page 185..

2 Place the embroidery hoop over the design and tighten the hoop, making sure you haven't caught the other side of the bag in the hoop.

3 Cut your pieces of rags into strips about ½–1in/ 1–2.5cm wide.

4 Following the design, push the rag rug hook through the fabric, then wrap the rag around the hook before pulling the hook and rag back through to the front. The end of the strip must be on the front of the work to stop the hooked rag unraveling.

5 Continue to hook all the way around the design, moving the embroidery hoop when required. Remember to bring the end of every strip through to the outside of the bag, and then start each new strip by bringing the end of it to the outside as well.

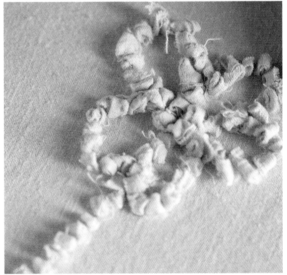

6 When you have hooked all of the design, finish off by bringing the end of the last strip through to the outside of the bag and then remove the embroidery hoop.

Braided seat pad

We've used a gorgeous vintage blanket and the technique of braiding (plaiting) to make this seat pad for an old French chair. Woolen blankets mean that frayed ends aren't an issue, joining the strips is easy, and the result is a thick, comfortable seat pad. This technique can easily be adapted to make a bigger mat or rug—just keep cutting and braiding the strips!

You will need

Old blanket

Scissors

Pins

Needle and thread

1 Cut the blanket into long strips about 2½in/7cm wide—keeping the strips long means you have to do less joining.

2 To join the strips together, cut a slot in one end of two strips of blanket—call them strip A and strip B.

The braided (plaited) seat pad turns a metal garden chair into somewhere comfortable to sit. Its spiral pattern echoes the sinuous lines of the chair.

3 Pass the uncut end of strip A through the slot of strip B to join the two strips together.

4 Pass the uncut end of B through the slot of the next strip. Continue joining all the strips together in this way until you have three strips, each one measuring 22ft/6.8m long.

5 Pin the ends of the three strips together and braid (plait) them by first bringing the left strip over the center one, then the right strip over the center. Continue braiding in this way until the braid measures about 15ft/4.5m long.

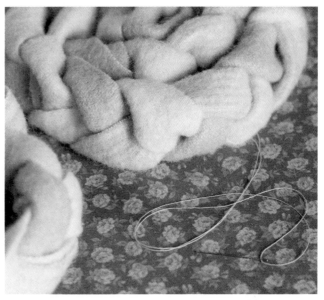

6 Remove the pin holding the beginning of the braid and secure the three ends together with a few stitches. Fold the combined end over by about 5in/13cm and sew right through the braid.

7 Start to coil the braid into a spiral to make the seat pad. Continue until the pad is the size you need for your chair, securing with stitches as you go.

8 When you have reached the desired size, cut the braid to neaten the ends and fold them in. Stitch in place.

Chapter Five

Natural Dyeing

Dyeing with plants is a craft that spans centuries, civilizations, and classes. The local plants used years ago can help historians to learn about how people in the past lived, traveled, and clothed themselves. The dyer, then and now, is both artist and scientist as the colors produced from the plant dyes can be altered by so many factors—the acidity of the water used, the time of year and age of the harvested plant material, and the mordants used to fix the dyes onto the fibers.

Animal fibers (silk and wool) will take up dye to give a much stronger shade than vegetable fibers (cotton and linen), which will take dye but the result will be quite pale in comparison and it is worth noting this when planning your dyeing. We've used madder (red), weld (yellow), purple common reed heads (green), and woad (blue) in the following recipes and based them on the techniques used by the Tudor dyers that take part in the Great Annual Re-Creation at Kentwell Hall in Suffolk.

The basics

Dyeing with plants doesn't mean that you are restricted to earthy shades. The following recipes show you how to use plants—woad, madder, weld, and reed heads—to produce vibrant and vivid shades of blue, red, yellow, and green. You can deepen shades by dyeing twice, and create new colors by dyeing first with one color and then with another. This is called over-dyeing.

You can influence the final color in a number of ways, which allows you to produce exactly the right shade. Copper pots, for example, will give a hint of blue/green, while iron pots will "sadden" (darken) the color. The mordant (see page 135), which fixes the dye, can also have an effect. Some plants do not produce the color you might expect. For example, the dye produced by purple feathery reed heeds is a deep shade of purple yet the resulting color is a rich pistachio green. Woad, on the other hand, a dark green leafy plant, produces a yellow dyebath and when the dyed items are removed and waved in the air they turn blue in front of your eyes!

Plants that produce dyes can be found growing in some surprising places. To find weld, which gives a bright yellow dye, you should look on waste grounds or even construction sites.

Types of dyes

Substantive dyes include woody ones, such as oak, which contain tannins—these will work as a natural mordant, or fixative. Rhubarb leaves with their high levels of oxalic acid that give a pale yellow dye, can also be used to pre-mordant fibers in preparation for dyeing with other colors. Adjective dyes will only fix onto the fiber when used with a mordant. The mordant can be applied to the fiber before and during dyeing and in some cases after dyeing. As the mordant chosen will have an effect on the resulting color, we've used alum to pre-mordant as it alters the color produced by the adjective dyes the least.

Substantive dyes

Woad is a substantive dye, which means that it can be used to dye wool (fabrics and yarns) that have not been pre-treated with a mordant. The seeds seen here are from woad. The beautiful blue dye that woad produces can be clearly seen on the seeds.

Adjective dyes

Madder, weld, and purple feathery common reed heads, however, are adjective dyes, and wool (fabrics and yarns) must be treated with a mordant before these dyes are applied. The mordant used will have an effect on the final color.

Mordants

Mordants help the dye to take, as well as stopping color from being washed out. There are many different kinds of mordant, all of which have an effect on the final shade. The mordant we have used in the recipes is alum (aluminum potassium sulfate), which alters the color the least. It is also considered by many dyers to be the safest to use.

Other mordants include copper sulfate, which helps produce blue/green shades and will brighten colours, and iron (ferrous sulfate), which will darken colors. Combined with walnut husks, iron produces black. Adding cream of tartar (potassium bitartrate) to the mordant bath will make the mordant more effective, but do not use it with madder, as it will "brown" the red.

The amount of of mordant used needs to be adjusted to suit the fiber. Animal fibers, such as wool or silk, take up dyes well, which means that they require less mordant, while plant fibers, like cotton or linen, need more. It is important to use the correct amount as too much could damage fibres and lead to a sticky feeling on the yarn.

Once the fiber has been treated with a mordant, it can be dried and stored for dyeing at a later date, as the required change has taken place by this point. The mordant changes the physical make up of the fibre so it cannot be rinsed off. The changes are not visible to the naked eye so labeling is advisable if you wish to keep items that have previously been mordanted in readiness for dyeing at another time.

Dry fibers take up mordant (and dyes) unevenly, which results in the finished dyed items appearing patchy. To avoid this, always soak fabrics or yarns for at least two hours before placing them in the mordant bath. When dyeing fibers with woad, the application of a mordant is not required. Soak the fibers for at least two hours before placing them in the dye bath. Soaking also prevents air from being introduced into the dye bath, which would stop the dye color developing.

The quantities shown (see right) are suitable for 2¼lb/1kg of animal fibre (wool or silk) and 1lb/500g of plant fiber (cotton or linen).

You will need

Fabric or yarn to be dyed

Water

4oz/100g alum

2 tsp cream of tartar (remove this ingredient when dyeing with madder)

Equipment

Large bowl or pail (bucket), for soaking and rinsing

Large pan

Old wooden spoon or stick, for removing the fabric or yarn

TAKE CARE

The mordant solution can be stored for use at a later date, but make sure that you label it clearly and store it out of the reach of children and pets. Always wear gloves when working with mordant, and don't breathe in any powder or fumes. Take care when disposing of any spent mordant. Keep it away from children, pets, fish ponds, and anywhere near where food stuffs are grown.

1 Soak the fabric or yarn in a large bowl or pail (bucket) containing plenty of cold water for at least 2 hours or, ideally, overnight.

2 Place the alum and cream of tartar (if using) in the pan and cover with boiling water, taking care not to breathe in any fumes. Dissolve the alum and cream of tartar, then top up with more water and bring to a gentle simmer.

3 If you are dyeing wool (fabric and yarn), prevent it from felting by placing it in a container of warm water (see Take Care box on page 130) to increase its temperature. Add the fabric or yarn to the mordant bath.

4 Bring back to a simmer and continue simmering gently for 20 to 30 minutes. Remove the pan from the heat. Place the items in a bowl or pail of warm water using the spoon or stick. Rinse well, making sure that there are no sudden changes in the temperature of the rinsing water. The fibers are now ready to dye or you can let them dry naturally for dyeing at a later date.

Weld

Weld (*Reseda luteola*) is a biennial plant that grows on rubbly, recently turned land. It gives a bright yellow dye but when overdyed with woad, it produces Lincoln green, which was supposedly worn by Robin Hood in Sherwood Forest. In Tudor times, weld-dyed cloth signified a single man who was seeking a partner.

If you have more weld than you need, you can dry it for future use. Hang up whole plants somewhere airy until they have dried, then break them up and store. If using dried weld for this recipe, you need to soak it overnight beforehand. The color achieved with dried weld is slightly duller than with fresh. Dried weld can also be bought from natural dye suppliers. Fabric and yarn will need to be treated with a mordant first. This recipe will dye up to 2¼lb/1kg of fiber.

You will need

1lb/454g fresh weld or 8oz/250g
dried weld, pre-soaked overnight
Sharp knife, if using fresh weld
Water
Items to be dyed, pre-treated with
a mordant (see page 135) and
pre-soaked for at least 2 hours

Equipment
Large pot
Colander
Large bowl, for reserving the liquid
and rinsing
Old wooden spoon or stick, for
removing the dyed items

Weld, also known as dyer's rocket, gives a vivid yellow dye when used fresh. It can also be used dried but the result isn't as vibrant.

1 If using fresh weld, simply chop it up into small pieces with the knife. Add the fresh weld or pre-soaked dried weld to the pot and cover with water.

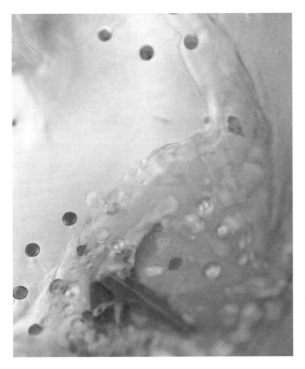

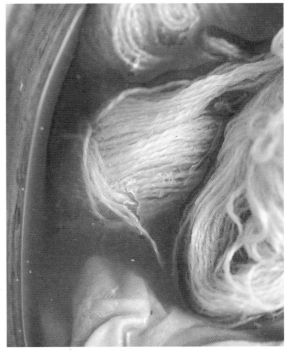

2 Bring to a simmer and continue to simmer gently until the dye bath is very yellow—this can take between five and 20 minutes. It is important not to overcook the weld, as the resulting color will be a sludgy green rather than a sunny yellow. Strain the cooked weld through a colander, reserving the liquid in the bowl. You can dry the weld to use for another dye batch, although it will give a paler shade.

3 Pour the liquid back into the pot and add the pre-soaked items you wish to dye. Make sure you warm any wool (fabric and yarn) before adding to the pot (see page 130) to prevent felting. Simmer gently until your fibers have reached a good color—this may take only five or ten minutes but it could be longer. Keep an eye on the color—if you simmer for too long, there is a danger of the items turning green.

FAST-ACTING DYE

This is a very quick-acting dye, so it's important to keep your eyes on the pot!

A glorious linen line of color! See how brightly the weld has dyed the linen bright yellow. Everyone is surprised to learn that a plant can produce such a color.

4 Remove the dyed items from the pot with the spoon or stick and place in the bowl. Rinse the items well in plenty of clean water before hanging out to dry.

Woad

Woad (*Isatis tinctoria*) is a leafy plant belonging to the brassica family, which also includes cabbages and broccoli. Watching anyone dyeing with woad is like watching a magician perform a magic trick, with spectacular color changes from yellow to green to blue taking place right before your eyes. It's a good idea to enlist some help when dyeing with woad because there is a lot of whisking involved in preparing the dye bath, and when the dyed items are taken out of the bath, they must be waved around in the air to encourage airflow.

There is no need to treat fabrics and yarn with a mordant before dyeing them with woad. This recipe will dye up to 2¼lb/1kg of fiber.

You will need

Items to be dyed
Water
1oz/25g woad powder
2oz/50g soda ash
2oz/50g thiourea dioxide
(Spectralite)

Equipment
Large bowl or pail (bucket), for
soaking and rinsing
Large pot
Spoon and small bowl, for mixing
the pastes
Hand whisk
pH test paper
Old wooden spoon or stick, for
removing the dyed items
Colander

1 Soak the items to be dyed in a bowl or pail of clean water for two hours. This will allow a good take-up of the dye and prevent air from being introduced into the dye bath.

2 Heat some water in the pot. While it is warming up, use the spoon to mix the woad powder with a little warm water in the small bowl—this will help the powder to dissolve more easily.

3 Thin the paste until it is fairly runny by adding a little more water. Pour into the pot of warmed (tepid) water.

4 In the same way, make a paste with the soda ash and add to the mixture.

5 Tip in the thiourea dioxide (Spectralite). This works with the soda ash to dissolve the woad powder.

6 Whisk for 20 minutes to help add oxygen to the solution. The foam on the top will be blue but the liquid underneath will be yellow.

7 Test the liquid with pH paper—the reading should be around 9. Keeping the solution warm on a low heat, let it rest for 20 minutes.

8 Add warm water to the bowl of soaking fibers to increase their temperature. Slide the warmed fibers gently down the side of the pot into the dye, taking care not to disturb the surface too much.

9 Leave the fibers submerged—we used an old pan lid that fitted inside our dye pot to help keep them below the surface. Keep covered for 20 minutes.

10 Lift the lid. You will see that the liquid and the dyed fibers are not yet blue but still very yellow—this is because the dye needs to react with oxygen to develop.

11 Remove the fibers carefully from the dye pot with the wooden spoon into the colander. Be very careful not to let liquid dribble back into the dye bath and disturb the surface—this stops oxygen entering the bath so that further dippings are possible, although you will get lighter shades of blue with each dipping.

12 Wave the fibers in the air for about 15 minutes to encourage airflow and help the oxygen react with the dye to develop the color. This is messy work and best done outdoors. The color change is very dramatic, going from yellow to green to dark blue in front of your eyes! Rinse the fibers well in plenty of clean water and hang out to dry.

Dyeing fleece

The fleece that we have dyed with is from Wensleydale sheep. It's very soft and has long fibers, which makes it lovely to spin with and it has none of the short fibers that can sometimes make wool itchy. Shake the fleece in the air and, while doing so, open it up so that as much

of it is exposed as possible—it is oxygen reacting with the dye that develops the color. The color change is dramatic and it will quickly start to change from the yellow shade to green and then finally to a lovely shade of blue. It takes around 15 minutes for the shade to

develop after which it can be rinsed in plenty of clean water before being left out to dry naturally. The fleece is now ready to use and is ideal for wet felting, needle felting, spinning, or weaving with.

Dyeing yarn

The yarn we have dyed with woad is 100% wool—being an animal fibre, it dyes very well with natural dyes. Before dyeing yarn, it needs to be put into skeins and tied in several places in order to stop it getting tangled during the dyeing process. Make sure that the ties are not too tight or the dye will not get onto all of the yarn and this will make the finished result patchy. The skeins of wool need to be removed carefully from the dye bath and at this stage will still be quite yellow but the color will start to change as soon as they emerge into the air. Keep the skeins of yarn moving for the 15 minutes that it takes for the color to develop, then rinse them in plenty

of clean water. Hang the skeins out to dry naturally. It is a good idea to give the yarn a gentle wash with some detergent that is suitable for wool before knitting anything with it.

Dyeing silk

Silk is an animal fiber, which means that it will take a dye well. It is fairly easy to handle and the sheen of silk really shows off the colors produced by the natural dyes. You can clearly see where the silk has come to the surface of the dye bath and the oxygen has already started to react with the dye and turned blue. It can be tricky to keep larger pieces of fabric moving so it is a good idea to have a bit of assistance during this stage of the woad dyeing. Don't wear your best clothes— aprons and old clothes are needed as the droplets of dye that come off will develop and you will soon discover that you are wearing a lot of tiny blue spots! When the color has developed fully (around 15 minutes), rinse the fabric in plenty of clean water and then hang out to dry.

Madder

It is the roots of the madder plant (*Rubia tinctorum*) that are used for dyeing. Since they are fibrous they need to be chopped into small pieces before being using and dried. Chopped madder is available from natural dye suppliers (see pages 188–9). The color obtained from madder is affected by a number of things, such as the temperature of the dye bath, the mordant used, and the items you wish to dye. A strong red can be obtained on yarn and silk, and paler pink shades on linen and cotton. Fabrics and yarn need to be treated with a mordant (see page 135) before they are dyed with madder, but leave out the cream of tartar from the ingredients because it will give the red a brown tinge. This recipe will dye up to 2¼lb/1kg of fiber.

You will need

1lb/454g dried madder
Water
Items to be dyed, pre-treated with a
mordant and pre-soaked for 2 hours

Equipment
Cheesecloth (muslin) bag to contain
the madder—it will double in size
during soaking
String, for tying the bag
Large pot
Old wooden spoon or stick, for
removing the dyed items

The dried roots of madder can produce colors from deepest red to palest pink.

1 Place the madder in the cheesecloth (muslin) bag. Tie the top closed with the string, making sure that there is room for the madder to swell up during soaking. Soak the whole bag overnight in the pot of cold water.

2 Heat the pan and simmer gently until the dye bath turns a deep red.

3 Remove the bag of madder and put to one side. Add the pre-soaked items to the dye bath—if you are dyeing wool (fabric and yarn), warm it beforehand (see Take Care box on page 130) to prevent felting. Simmer gently, as boiling the dye bath may cause browning.

4 Remove the dyed items from the pot with the spoon. Rinse them well in plenty of clean warm water, before hanging up to dry. You can use the dye bath again but it will give a paler shade. The spent madder can also be reused because it will still contain dye, although it will give a paler shade. Remove it from the bag and spread it out to dry.

HARD AND SOFT WATER

If your water is hard, you can get some really good, bright reds from madder root but it is not so easy with soft water. Adding some chalk to the dye bath may help.

Purple common reed heads

The common reed (*Phragmites australis*) is a wetland plant but an invasive one, so cultivation is controlled in many places. Their feathery heads are so purple that you would never guess that the color they give is a rich pistachio-green! The best time to collect the heads for dyeing is when they are a glossy purple, just before they flower in high summer. Using a copper pot for the dyeing helps to brighten the shade of green.

Fabrics and yarns will need to be treated with a mordant before they are dyed with reed heads. This recipe will dye up to 2¼lb/1kg of fiber.

You will need

About 2 large handfuls of reed heads
Water
Items to be dyed, pre-treated with
a mordant and pre-soaked for
2 hours or overnight

Equipment
Large pot
Colander
Large bowl, for reserving the liquid
and rinsing
Old wooden spoon or stick, for
removing the dyed items

Purple, feathery common reed heads, ready to be simmered in water. Surprisingly, the color they produce is a rich pistachio-green.

2 Place the reed heads in the pot, cover with water, and simmer. The water will turn red. Continue to simmer until you can see no further darkening of the water.

1 Strain the reed heads through a colander, reserving the liquid in the bowl. Dispose of the reed heads, ideally on the compost heap, as they can't be used again. Pour the liquid back into the pot and add the presoaked items to the dye bath—if you are dyeing wool (fabric and yarn), warm it beforehand (see Take Care box on page 130) to prevent felting.

COLOR CHECK

Check that the reed heads have finished changing the color of the water (see step 1) by dipping in a white cup and scooping out some of the liquid. Repeat every couple of minutes until there is no obvious visible change in color.

3 Simmer gently until the desired shade is reached or until there is no further color change. Remove the dyed items from the dye bath with the spoon or stick and place in the bowl. Rinse them well in plenty of clean warm water, then hang them up to dry. You can use the dye bath again but it will give a paler shade

Chapter Six

Reinvent

A passion for crafts, coupled with a desire to rescue and reuse discarded or out-of-fashion vintage items, gave us the idea for this chapter. Full of creative possibilities, it shows how the mundane and ordinary, such as men's shirts, tin trays, lace doilies, picture frames, and linen napkins, can be transformed into something new, beautiful, and unique but still with a useful purpose. The emphasis here is on being thrifty, without compromising on quality or style!

We're sure the projects in this chapter will spark your imagination. To help you along the way, you will find lots of ideas for varying the projects, and tips for using alternative found items, to personalize your creations. Enjoy the satisfaction that comes with creating something beautiful from a previously unwanted or unloved item!

Bunting from old shirts

Bunting is a lovely way to decorate your home and garden. Unlike paper garlands, a little rain will not ruin bunting because, when the sun comes out again, it will gently dry. Bunting may fade a little over time but we think that just makes it better-looking, and if it's made from old and unwanted clothes, it's a great way of recycling. We used a selection of men's old shirts and kept to a theme of red, white, and blue, one of our favorite color combinations. The instructions below are for bunting about 3 yards/3m long but you can make it any length you like—just leave enough tape at each end with which to tie it up.

You will need

Template (see page 186)
Old shirts
Tailor's chalk or soft pencil
Scissors
Pins
Sewing machine with thread to match
the tape or ribbon
3 yards/3m of tape or ribbon,
1in/2.5cm wide
Tape measure

1 Using the template as a guide, mark and cut out the triangles from the shirts. This bunting is double-sided, so you will need two triangles for each "flag." Cut out 18 triangles in total.

2 Place the triangles in pairs, wrong sides facing, and pin together. Machine-stitch the two long sides of each pair, ½in/1cm in from the edge.

Bunting is probably the most public way to announce a celebration. Easy to make to any length you like, you can stretch it across a garden gate or the entire width of a house.

3 When you have sewn all the triangles together, lay them out in front of you to see in what order they will look best when sewn onto the tape or ribbon.

4 Select tape or ribbon in a coordinating color—we used old seam binding but a grosgrain ribbon would look nice, too.

5 Fold the tape in half along its length and pin together for about 12in/30cm—this will be for tying up your bunting.

6 Place the unsewn side of the first flag within the fold of the tape after the pins. Pin the tape and flag together.

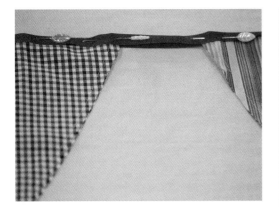

7 Continue pinning the flags in place in the same way, leaving a gap of about 3in/7.5cm between each one. After the last flag, there should be 12in/30cm of tape left. Fold and pin this length in the same way as the other end of the tape.

8 Machine-stitch along the entire length of the tape as closely as you can to the unfolded edge, making sure that the flags are securely in place.

VARIATIONS

Experiment with putting together different patterns as well as colors for the bunting, and perhaps include details such as buttons and buttonholes for a quirky and interesting note.

An old tin tray has been painted and given a new lease of life as a memo board. Fabric-covered buttons with magnetic backs keep important messages in place.

Magnetic memo board

Here's a fantastic way to give an old tin tray a new lease of life. The tray is a lovely shape and looks so pretty hanging from the gingham ribbon, yet it still retains a useful purpose as a memo, or bulletin, board! To finish off the project, we've shown you how to make fabric button magnets.

You will need

For the memo board

Tin tray

Wire wool (fine grade)

Tack rag or soft cloth

Paintbrush

Linseed oil paint or other paint suitable for metal, as a base coat

Linseed oil paint or other paint suitable for metal, as a top coat

Tracing paper

Pencil

Stencil template (see page 187)

Waxed card

Craft knife

Self-healing cutting mat

Paper towel

Craft mount spray

Ruler

Linseed or acrylic paints for stencil

Stencil brush

Artist's fixative spray

Clear wax (optional)

Soft cloth (optional)

Scissors

Ribbon, about 30in/76cm long

Stick-and-stick Velcro

For the button magnets

Self-cover buttons, ¾in/22mm diameter

Pair of pliers

Scraps of fabric, thin enough to fit into the button maker

Button maker

Needle and thread

Magnetic strip, ½-in/1-cm wide

Scissors

Glue, suitable for use on metal and rubber

1 Key the surface of the tray with wire wool to give a rough surface suitable for painting. Wipe the tray well with a tack rag or soft cloth so that it is clean and dust-free.

2 With a paintbrush, apply a thin base coat of linseed oil paint, following the manufacturer's instructions. Once this has dried thoroughly, apply two to three coats of your chosen top color. Allow to dry in accordance with the manufacturer's instructions. Sand lightly with the wire wool and wipe with the tack rag in between coats.

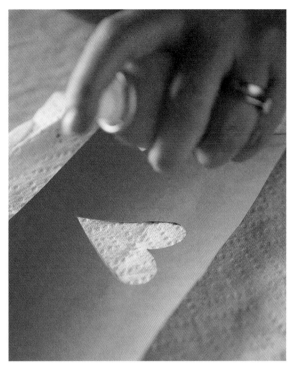

3 Trace the stencil design template (see page 187) onto waxed card and cut out with a craft knife on a cutting mat. Alternatively, you could trace the design directly onto your tray rather than cutting out a stencil.

4 Lay the stencil onto some paper towel, reverse side up, and spray on a small amount of craft mount. Let it become tacky (this will take a minute or so), then place it centrally on the tray, using the ruler as a guide.

BUYING STENCILS
If you don't want to cut your own stencil, buy one premade (see pages 188–9) for recommendations). Instead of a stencil, you could use découpage or a rubber stamp.

5 Apply a small amount of stencil paint to the tip of the stencil brush. Dab the brush in a stippling action on some paper towel to remove most of the paint, leaving the brush almost dry (too much paint will bleed under the edges of the stencil and spoil the design).

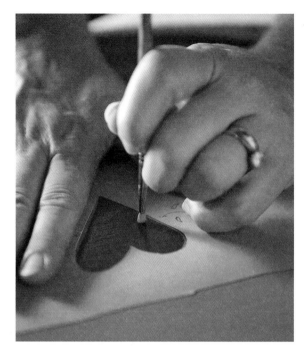

6 Apply the paint to the surface of the tray in a stippling
action, starting at the center of the stencil and working out
to the edges. If the paint needs a second coat, let the first coat
dry with the stencil in situ before applying, otherwise it may be
difficult to reposition the stencil in the right place.

7 Let the stenciled design dry completely, then spray a light
covering of artist's fixative over it, to seal the design.

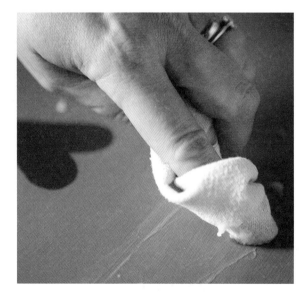

PAINT ALTERNATIVES

*Linseed oil paint is eco-friendly as well as suitable for use
on metal. If you're unable to find any, make sure that the
paint you use is suitable for metal and always follow
the manufacturer's instructions for safe use.*

8 Once the fixative has dried, apply some clear wax to the
entire surface of the tray with a soft cloth. Let the wax dry for
30 minutes or so and then buff to a soft sheen with a soft cloth.
The wax coating is not absolutely necessary but it will provide a
protective seal and your tray will last longer.

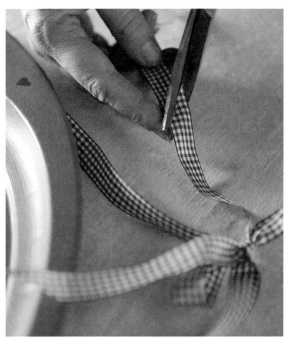

9 To make the hanger, cut the ribbon into two equal lengths. Cut a piece of stick-and-stick Velcro (the length will depend on the surface area of the tray), fixing one side to the left of center (take a measurement from the center point) on the reverse of the tray and the other to the ribbon. Repeat the process with the second length of ribbon, this time attaching it to the right of center of the tray. Make sure the measurement is the same as before, so that your tray is level when you hang it.

10 Tie the two pieces of ribbon together in a bow. Cut the ends on the diagonal for a professional finish.

FINISHING TOUCH

A ribbon bow means that you can alter the hanging height of your memo board, while Velcro means that you can remove the ribbon and still use the board as a tray!

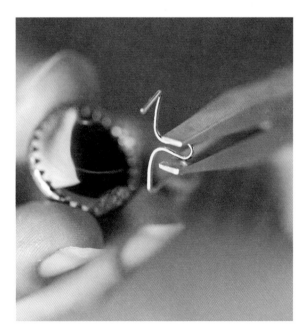

11 To make the button magnets, remove the shank from the back of each self-cover button with pliers.

12 Draw around the gauge supplied with the button maker and cut out a corresponding circle of fabric.

13 Insert the fabric circle into the button maker, right side down, then place the button dome on top of the fabric.

14 Gather the edges of the fabric circle together with a needle and thread.

15 Place the button back onto the other half of the button maker and bring the two together, pressing firmly until you hear them snap into place.

17 Use scissors to cut a length of magnet to cover the back of the button but without it showing from the front. Apply glue to the magnet and stick to the finished button.

16 Pop the finished button out of the button maker.

> ## VARIATIONS
>
> *Instead of self-cover buttons, use vintage or decorative buttons and glue a small magnet to the back.*

18 Repeat until you have the desired number of buttons for the board.

Ribbon invitation board

There are an infinite number of fabric bulletin boards available to buy premade but why not make one from recycled or secondhand store finds to reflect both your home and your personality instead? Let your creativity run wild with this easy-to-do project and have the satisfaction of creating something unique at a fraction of the cost of a store-bought version.

You will need

Picture frame
Piece of denim or linen (needs to
exceed size of picture frame by
3–4in/10cm all around)
Ruler
Tailor's chalk or vanishing marker
pen
Staple gun
Scissors
Selection of ribbons and rickrack
Decorative buttons
Needle and thread

NEAT CORNERS

Mitering your corners before stapling all the fabric to the frame will make it much easier to manipulate the fabric into a neat finish (see step 4).

1 Remove the image, glass, and any backing from the picture frame. Lay the frame face down on the fabric. With a ruler and tailor's chalk or marker pen, mark the fabric as a guide when cutting, remembering to add 3–4in/10cm all around for turning the fabric to size.

2 Fold over the edges of the fabric twice, to give a neat finish.

3 Staple the fabric to the frame at the center point of one side of the frame. Do the same on the opposite side to keep the tension even. Repeat this process on the two remaining sides, then staple the fabric to the frame at regular intervals all around, ensuring you keep the fabric taut as you go.

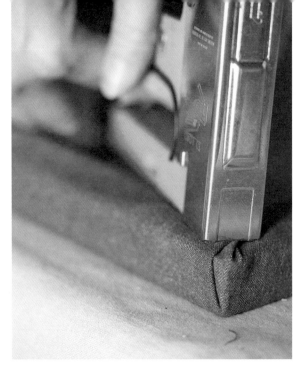

4 To remove the bulk of unwanted fabric at the corners, cut out a V-shape at each corner, making sure that you don't cut too close to the frame.

5 Fold over the fabric where you made the cuts to make neat mitered corners and staple in place.

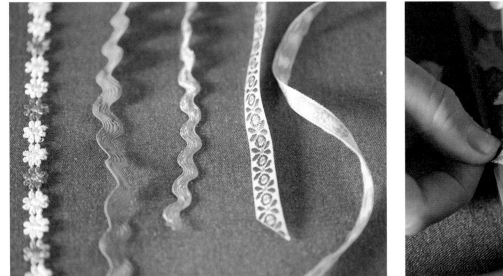

6 Turn the bulletin board right side up. Place a selection of ribbons and rickrack on top and play with their position until you are happy with the design and order. The spacing is really up to you but, as a guide, allow about ½in/1cm between each piece.

7 Staple one end of a piece of ribbon to the back of the board, using a ruler to help with the spacing if necessary.

8 Take the ribbon across the front of the board and onto the reverse of the other side. Make sure your spacing is accurate and that the ribbon is straight. Pull the ribbon taut before stapling it to the frame. Cut any excess ribbon.

9 Continue to add ribbons and rickrack in this way until you have covered the entire board.

10 As a final flourish, sew some decorative buttons onto the ribbon and rickrack at irregular intervals.

Linen napkin silverware roll

Why not rediscover a sense of occasion with these sophisticated additions to your dining table? For this extremely simple project, we have transformed a set of vintage cutwork napkins into silverware rolls, ideal for summer picnics as well as formal dining. You need very few supplies, and there is a good chance you already have some linen napkins tucked away in a drawer. Even if you don't, you can find plenty of lovely, relatively inexpensive examples in secondhand or thrift (charity) stores.

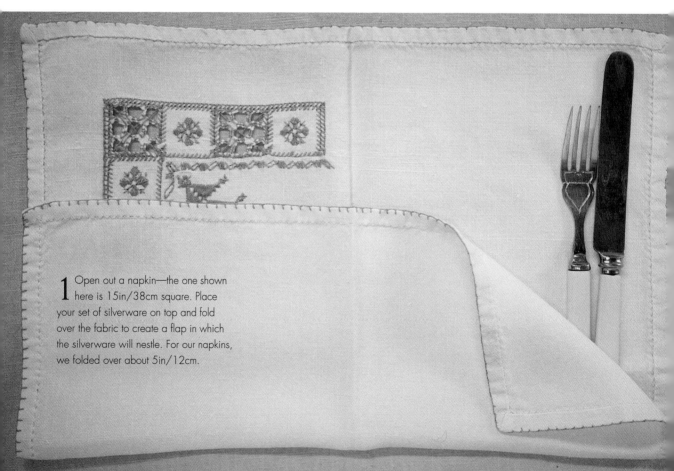

1 Open out a napkin—the one shown here is 15in/38cm square. Place your set of silverware on top and fold over the fabric to create a flap in which the silverware will nestle. For our napkins, we folded over about 5in/12cm.

You will need

Linen napkins

Silverware

Tape measure

Velvet ribbon, about ½in/1cm wide

Pin

Buttons, one for each napkin

Needle and thread

Scissors

2 With the silverware tucked inside the fold, roll up the napkin loosely to form a sausage so you can work out how much ribbon you need for the tie.

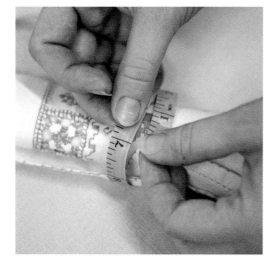

3 Wrap the tape measure loosely around the roll. Note the measurement and double it. Then add 6in/15cm to allow for the "tails"— these are purely decorative and give a pretty finish. Cut the ribbon accordingly. For these napkins, we used velvet ribbon 18in/45cm long.

Transform any table setting with these gorgeous silverware rolls, made from vintage linen napkins. As well as costing next to nothing, they are also incredibly simple to make.

4 Fold the ribbon in half to form a loop and wrap it around the roll. With a pin, mark the point at which the loop of the ribbon meets the other end. This is where you will place the button that forms the fastening.

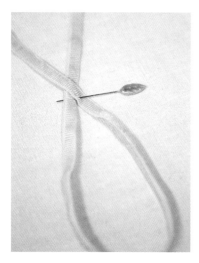

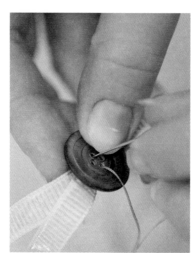

BUTTONS

Take time to choose some special buttons from your collection to add a lovely personal finish to your project.

5 Remove the ribbon from the napkin roll and fan out the ends a little to provide the decorative "tails."

6 Sew a button onto the ribbon where marked with the pin, at the crossover point.

VARIATION

Use mismatched napkins in similar patterns or complementary tones for a quirky look.

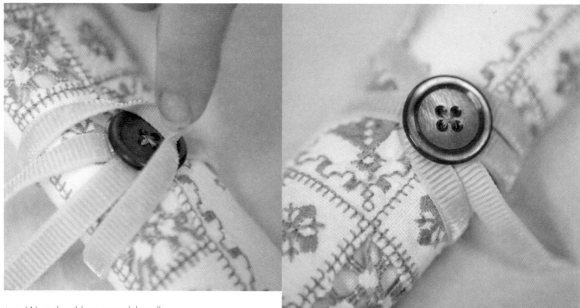

7 Wrap the ribbon around the roll, passing the loop over the button to fasten securely. For a professional finish, snip the ribbon ends on the diagonal.

Sophisticated linen napkin silverware rolls turn a simple summer picnic into a much more glamorous affair.

Beaded covers

The start point for these gorgeous beaded pitcher (jug) covers is a crocheted lace doily—these delightful little works of art come in all manner of designs and have, over the years, been crafted with much care and love, yet in recent times they have fallen out of fashion. Here's a great way to reinvent and reuse pretty doilies, with myriad possibilities for you to personalize them. With just the bare minimum of supplies you can create something truly unique. We've used a variety of vintage and contemporary buttons, beads, and findings to give you inspiration—but whether you use what you already have or choose to purchase something to complement your décor, you are bound to be pleased with your finished handiwork!

You will need

Vintage lace or crocheted doily
Beads or buttons
Needle
Embroidery thread in cream or
white, as close in color to the doily
as possible
Scissors

CHOOSING BEADS

Let the shape, pattern, style, and size of your doily help inform your choice of button or bead.

Vintage lace doilies have been given a new lease of life as pitcher covers, decorated with beads and buttons to hold them in place.

1 Spread the doily flat on your work surface. Decide upon the type and number of beads or buttons you will need by looking at the natural edge of your doily— there may be points to which you can attach them or you may wish to position them to work with a certain pattern repeat. The number of beads or buttons needed will depend on the size of your doily and the size and weight of your beads may influence the number you use—as a guide, we have used 10–20 on the designs shown here.

2 Sew each of your chosen beads or buttons onto the doily using a needle and embroidery thread.

3 Once you have sewn on the beads or buttons, put your finished cover into use!

Templates

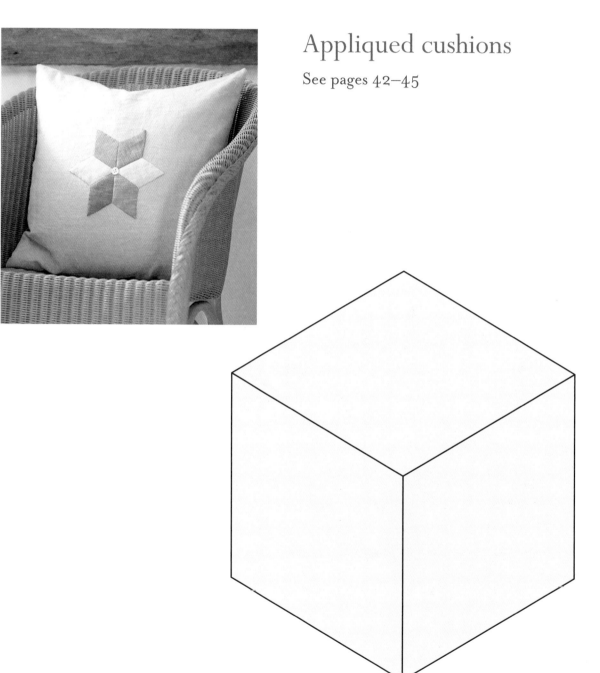

Appliqued cushions

See pages 42–45

Decorative hooked
flower motif

See pages 120–123

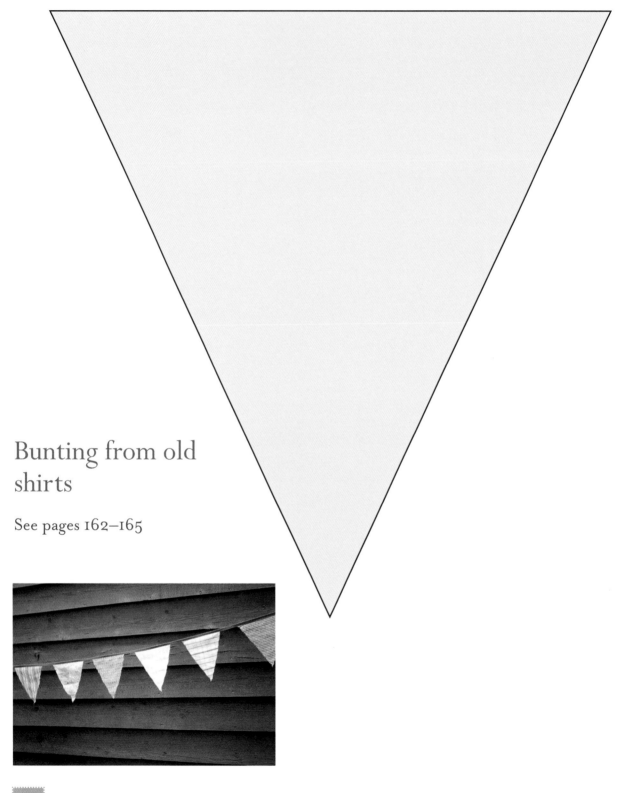

Bunting from old shirts

See pages 162–165

Magnetic memo board

See pages 166–173

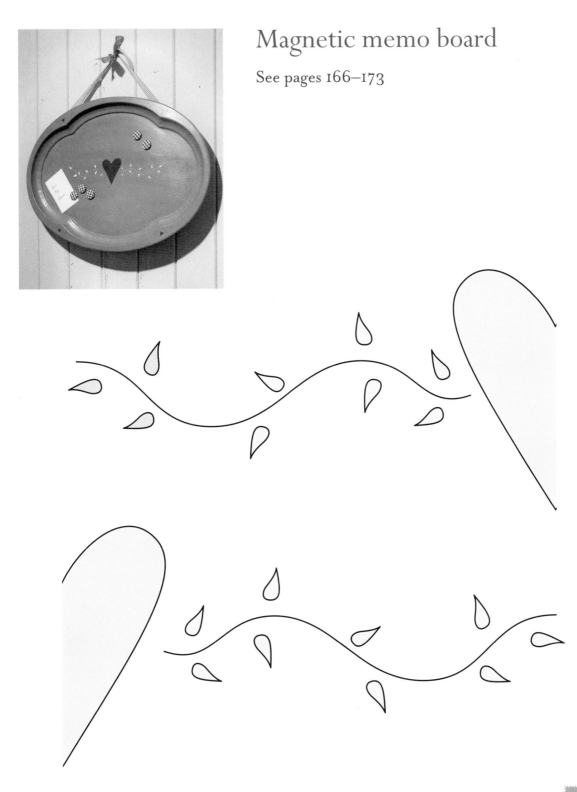

Useful addresses

Halfpenny Home
3 Station Yard
Needham Market
Suffolk
IP6 8AS
Tel: 01449 720468
www.halfpennyhome.co.uk
For all manner of
haberdashery along with
fabrics, trimmings, crafting
supplies, and tools

Local charities
Support your local charity
(thrift) shops to save money
and reduce the amount of
useable, although no longer
wanted items, ending up
in landfill. By buying
second- hand goods you are
helping other people, the
environment, and yourself.
Our local UK charity shop
is Sue Ryder. To find out
about them and the work
that they do, go to
www.suerydercare.org

NORTH AMERICA

Bramble Berry®
2138 Humboldt St.
Bellingham
WA 98225
Tel: 877 627 7883
www.brambleberry.com
For soap-making supplies

Candles & Supplies
500 Commerce Drive
Quakertown
PA 18957
Tel: 215-538-8552
www.candlesandsupplies.com

Crafts etc
Tel: 1-800-888-0321
www.craftsetc.com

Hobby Lobby
www.hobbylobby.com

Ikea
www.ikea.com
For kilner jars and other
reasonably priced containers

Michaels
1-800-642-4235

Soap Making Essentials
PO Box 197
Sicamous, BC, V0E 2V0
Canada
www.soap-making-essentials.
com

Winsor & Newton
11 Constitution Avenue
Piscataway

New Jersey 08854
Tel: 800-445-4278
www.winsornewton.com

The Woolery
239 West Main Street
Frankfort
KY 40601
Tel: 800 441 9665
www.woolery.com

The Yarn Tree
347 Bedford Avenue
Brooklyn
New York
NY 1121
Tel: 718 384 8030
www.theyarntree.com

UK
Denny Bros Supplies Ltd
50 St Andrews Street North
Bury St Edmunds
Suffolk
IP33 3PH
www.dennybrosshops.co.uk
For art materials

The Gedgrave Flock
Tel: 01394 450343
For Wensleydale fleece
and yarns
Gentil Sayre Ltd,
Unit 3A-C,
Beacon Road
Withernsea
East Yorks
HU19 2EG
Tel: 0871 200 2087
www.4candles.co.uk
For candle-making supplies

George Weil and Sons Ltd
Old Portsmouth Road
Peasmarsh
Guildford
Surrey
GU3 1LZ
Tel 01483 565800
www.fibrecrafts.com
For natural dyes and
mordants

Gracefruit Limited
Tel: 07772 908087
www.gracefruit.com
For soapmaking supplies

Hobbycraft
www.hobbycraft.co.uk

Holkham Linseed Paints
The Clock Tower
Longlands
Holkham
Wells-Next-The-Sea
NR23 1RU
Tel: 01328 711348
www.holkhamlinseedpaints.
co.uk

Ikea
www.ikea.co.uk
For kilner jars and other
reasonably priced containers
John Lewis
Tel: 08456 049 049
www.johnlewis.com

Knit collage
Shop 1, G/F
Po Hing Fong Court
10-18 Po Hing Fong
Sheung Wan. Hong Kong
+852 2389 6395

www.knitcollage.com
For handspun speciality yarns

Piggery Pottery
Alder Carr Farm
Needham Market
Suffolk
IP6 8LX
Tel: 01449 721166
http://piggerypottery.co.uk/
For handmade ceramic
buttons and beads

For Purdy paintbrushes
www.amazon.co.uk and
www.purdycorp.com for
more stockists.

Teresinha Roberts
www.woad.org.uk
A great supplier for woad,
spectralite, and soda ash

The Stencil Library
Stocksfield Hall
Stocksfield
Northumberland
NE43 7TN
Tel: 01661 844 844
www.stencil-library.co.uk

Vintage French
Green Farm Lodge
Menlesham Green
Stowmarket
Suffolk
IP14 5RE
Tel: 01449 766336
www.vintagefrench.co.uk
For vintage linen and fabrics

Winsor & Newton
Whitefriars Avenue
Harrow
Middlesex
HA3 5RH
Tel: 020 8424 3200
www.winsornewton.com
For art materials

Index

Acknowledgments

Our thanks go to Gavin Kingcome for his lavish and beautiful photography, which has ensured our projects have been brought to life. Thanks to all at CICO and, in particular, Cindy Richards, who suggested the idea for the book and for having the belief in us.

Thank you to Sam Hayes for providing her expertise, support and help with the Dyeing chapter and to Laura for her recipes, guidance, and time in preparing and providing the soap recipes.

To the generous and kind friends who let us invade their homes and gardens for use as locations: Harriet Fear for the use of her beautiful home, to Julie and Bernie Andrews for the use of their very special home, garden, and private shoreline, and to The Curtain Agency, Needham Market.

A special thank you to Val Beeson for her continuing support, advice, and for the use of her lovely home and garden.

Thank you to the good wives of "sew and crow" for their endless support and inspiration.

Finally to our loved ones, you know who you are, for supporting us throughout.